MARX
IN LONDON
An Illustrated Guide

ASA BRIGGS
with
John Dekker and John Mair

British Broadcasting Corporation

Published by the
British Broadcasting Corporation
35 Marylebone High Street
London W1M 4AA

ISBN 0 563 20076 6

First published 1982
© Asa Briggs 1982

Printed in England by
Jolly & Barber Ltd, Rugby

This book is published in conjunction with
the BBC–Television programme
Karl Marx in London, produced by
John Mair and presented by Asa Briggs.
First broadcast in the summer of 1982.

The photograph on the title page shows a detail
from Marx's tomb in Highgate Cemetery,
London

Acknowledgements and Picture Credits
The authors would like to thank Judy Andrews for research and much else, Chris Capstick and Philip
Carr for photographs, and Victoria Huxley, Veronica Loveless and Desmond Green of BBC
Publications.

The daguerreotype on page 19 (bottom) is reproduced by gracious permission of Her Majesty the
Queen.

BARNABY'S PICTURE LIBRARY pages 67, 79, 81; BBC HULTON PICTURE LIBRARY pages 6 (both), 7, 8 (top),
9, 12 (bottom), 13 (bottom), 14 (top), 16, 19 (top), 23, 24 (left), 30 (both), 32 (right), 41 (top), 49, 55,
57 (bottom), 61, 68 (top), 69, 72 (right), 73 (top), 80, 83 (top right), 92 (bottom right); BRITISH LIBRARY
page 48 (bottom); TRUSTEES OF THE BRITISH MUSEUM pages 44, 46 (both); CAMDEN PUBLIC LIBRARIES
page 62; CHRIS CAPSTICK pages 22, 34 (both), 36, 37, 38, 39, 40, 45; PHILIP CARR pages 42 (right), 52, 53
(both); DAILY TELEGRAPH COLOUR LIBRARY title page; DIETZ VERLAG pages 27 (top), 31 (bottom); JOHN
GORMAN page 68 (bottom); GREATER LONDON COUNCIL PHOTO LIBRARY page 92 (top, and bottom left);
THE GUARDIAN page 25; DAVID HEISLER page 84 (right); ILLUSTRATED LONDON NEWS pages 12/13 (top),
47; INTERNATIONAL INSTITUTE OF SOCIAL HISTORY, AMSTERDAM pages 28, 42 (left), 59; JAMES KLUGMANN
COLLECTION pages 8 (bottom), 33, 73 (bottom), 83 (top left), 89 (top left), 90; MANCHESTER PUBLIC
LIBRARIES page 41 (bottom); MANSELL COLLECTION pages 20, 21, 24 (right), 29, 31 (top), 64 (bottom),
72 (left), 89 (top right), 91 (top); MARX INSTITUTE, EAST BERLIN pages 63 (top), 72; MARX MEMORIAL
LIBRARY pages 33 (left), 38 (left), 48 (top), 56 (both), 57 (top), 58, 63 (bottom), 64 (top), 75, 76 (right),
83 (bottom), 84 (left), 89 (bottom), 91 (bottom); MUSEUM OF LONDON page 18; NATIONAL RAILWAY
MUSEUM, YORK page 14 (bottom); POPPERFOTO pages 76 (left) – U.P.I., 78; SCIENCE MUSEUM, LONDON
pages 15, 54; TRANSPORT & GENERAL WORKERS UNION page 88; TRIER TOWN MUSEUM page 10; ULLSTEIN
BILDERDIENST pages 26, 27 (bottom).

Maps by Line and Line.

Contents

1
The English Connection

Karl Marx was born in the ancient German city of Trier in 1818, one year before Queen Victoria. Thirty-one years later, he settled in London as an exile – he had already visited it as a revolutionary – and remained there until his death in 1883. Queen Victoria was to live on into the twentieth century – until 1901 – a century when Marx's influence was to extend throughout the world, and the Victorian Empire to disappear.

This booklet is concerned with Marx's English – and specifically, London – connection, which was always more than geographical in character. It has often been said that Marx acquired his philosophy in Germany, his politics in France and his economics in England. Although this is one of the many over-simplifications about him, there is no doubt that he set about studying and explaining the laws of political economy and how, in his view, they would lead to working-class revolution, in what was then the most prosperous city in the world.

Thousands of visitors to late-twentieth century London are interested in seeing the places with which Marx was particularly associated. This booklet is intended for them. It is designed to be of interest also to readers who are concerned to find out more about the life of Marx

himself. It sets out useful information, both biographical and topographical and is fully-illustrated with photographs and maps which show how the places which Marx knew have changed since his death in 1883. It deals also with some of Marx's successors, notably Lenin, and their own connection with London.

Although in the twentieth century Marx's name is everywhere associated with that of Lenin, in his lifetime it was most frequently linked with that of his fellow German revolutionary Friedrich Engels, who was born two years after Marx and died – also in London – twelve years after him. It was Engels who not only supplied Marx with indispensable financial support but, before coming to London, with an invaluable connection with industrial Manchester.

London was then the world's great capital city. Some thought of it, indeed, as the capital of the world. Yet Manchester the most conspicuous of the new industrial cities of the nineteenth century, was a shock city which everyone who wished to understand what was happening to society in the age of steam felt compelled to visit. Engels's own book *The Condition of the Working Class in England* was based on his impressions of life in Manchester and his reading. In focusing on the textile

The New Bailey Bridge, Manchester, around 1830

industry, the source of Manchester's wealth, and on the class struggle, as Engels saw it, between employers and workers, it was directly related to the economic and political analysis in Marx's own work.

There were many foreign political exiles in Manchester, particularly following the failure of the European revolutions of 1848, but before and after that date, London was the place in England where most of them congregated. Some came in singly; others in waves. Not all of them were revolutionaries, however. Indeed, Metternich, Europe's leading anti-revolutionary, fled for safety from Vienna to London after the revolutions of 1848, while Louis Napoleon, later Napoleon III, was a British special constable, enrolled during the Chartist disturbances of that same year. Later in the century, the American novelist, Henry James, a very different kind of exile, was to describe

London as 'an epitome of the round world'.

Nineteenth-century London is usually referred to in our own century as Victorian

Napoleon III, the French Emperor

London, with distinctions being drawn between early, middle, and late Victorian moods and styles. But it has also been described, rightly, as the London of Charles Dickens, and many of today's visitors, including those particularly interested in Marx, often start with a picture of Dickens's London in mind. Indeed no other single writer has done more to perpetuate in his writings the sense of Victorian London than Dickens, who lived from 1812 to 1870. Yet it is important to realise, first, that his pictures of London were paintings, not photographs, and, second, that London changed greatly, both during his own lifetime and, even more, between 1870 and 1901. To discover what remains of Dickens's London requires as much exploration, preferably on foot, as does the discovery of the London of Marx.

This booklet is an invitation to explore and is based on our own exploration of the city. But although every explorer will draw his own map, and no two maps are quite alike, it is hoped that this guide will prove useful to all.

Certainly London provoked ambivalent reactions on the part of the exiles who settled here in the nineteenth century. Thus, Alexander Herzen, the Russian revolutionary, who arrived in London in 1852, complained three years later that London life was 'about as boring as that of worms in a cheese'. Yet two years after that he told a Swiss friend, 'beyond all manner of doubt, England, with all the follies of Feudalism and Toryism which are peculiar to it, is the only country to live in'.

Seven features of London are of major importance.

1: the River Thames, so important a stimulus to the imagination of Dickens; the river had for centuries shaped London's history, linking the city with Europe but dividing north from south.

2: the sharp contrast, already apparent in the 1840s, between metropolitan east and west, a contrast of poverty and privilege which was sharpened during the century.

3: the City, centre of the world's banking

Charles Dickens, the novelist

and commerce, with its own jurisdiction.

4: the presence outside the City, in Westminster and Whitehall, of centres of power, particularly Parliament, which were also – through the working of a political system different from that of Marx's Germany – symbols of freedom.

5: the British Museum, as much of a powerhouse of knowledge for Marx as the mills of Manchester were a powerhouse for Britain's first generations of industrialists.

6: the visual variety of London. Unlike the Paris of Napoleon III, London was not planned on a large scale. There had long been building regulations, and it had its eighteenth-century squares and terraces, parts of aristocratic estates, but it lacked the great boulevards of Paris. Nash had left his imprint on London (Regent Street, for example and Regent's Park), but there was no counterpart of Baron Haussman. Londoners wanted it to be so.

7: 'outcast London', the London of the

'dangerous classes'. In the 1860s they lived in close proximity to the rich. By the end of the century, however, they were increasingly segregated. By then, too, there had been an outward movement into both working-class and middle-class suburbia.

Most Londoners had never heard of Marx by the time that he died, and even socialists – some of them emerging from the most deprived districts of the city – usually would have little to do with his programme. Yet he shared many of their common experiences. His daughter, Eleanor (1855–1898) was a British citizen, and he himself applied for naturalisation, and was refused it, in 1874.

William Liebknecht (1826–1900), who knew the Marx family well, has given a graphic account of change in Victorian London in his book *Karl Marx: Biographical Memoirs* (1896). Having first lived in London as a political exile during the 1850s, Liebknecht returned from Germany in 1878, comparing himself with

William Liebknecht, a close friend of the Marx family

the archaeologist Schliemann when he set out to excavate Troy. He immediately discerned that the revolution which had taken place since he had been in London before was topographical, not ideological,

and he was prepared to generalise from it: 'What revolutionary changes in the modern great cities,' he observed. 'It is a continual uprooting – although, as in political revolutions also, not everywhere, not in all parts. And a man starting today from a modern great city on a tour of the world will not be able on his return to find his way through a good many quarters.'

On arriving back in London after an absence of sixteen years, Liebknecht went on, he had rubbed his eyes, 'Was this the city in which I have lived for nearly half a generation and of which I then knew every street, every corner?' he asked, 'Streets gone, sections disappeared – new streets, new buildings, and the general aspect so changed that in a place where I formerly could have made my way blindfolded I had to take refuge in a cab in order to get to my near goal.'

There must have been many visitors to late-Victorian London who shared Liebknecht's reactions. Not everywhere

had changed, however, and Liebknecht ended his tour on Hampstead Heath, lunching at the public house, Jack Straw's Castle. 'How many hundred times had we been here. And in the same room where we were sitting today, I had been sitting – long, long ago – dozens of times with Marx, with Mrs Marx, with the children, with Lenchen, the family maid, and others. And the past returned.'

When Marx came to London in 1849, his own past involved very different German associations – the old city of Trier, surrounded by vineyards and wooded hills, once a Roman headquarters; the university town of Bonn; Berlin, capital of Prussia. But there were non-German elements in his experience too. Paris, itself a city of wealth (and corruption) in the 1840s, was as brilliantly described by his favourite novelist, Balzac, as London was by Dickens, and it was a city associated with revolution, as London was not. Brussels was the capital of a newly-formed Belgian

The market town of Trier in the Rhineland, where Marx was born

Kingdom, where there was substantial early industrialisation, as in Britain.

Marx was now separated physically from that experience, but he never became so preoccupied with London – or England – that the English connection changed his attitudes and his feelings. It provided him with data and with ideas – and with basic security to study and to live – but for the application of what he found out he always looked to a far wider scene. Immediately after his arrival, however, he assured a friend that 'a tremendous industrial, agricultural and commercial crisis was approaching in England' and that 'even against its will' England could become 'an ally of the revolutionary continent'.

2
The London Marx Found

The London Marx came to in 1849 was already a huge city of two-and-a-half million people, the biggest city in the world, a vast built-up area stretching nine miles from Fulham in the west to the riverside town of Poplar in the east, and seven miles from Highbury in the north to Camberwell in the south.

It was still largely a Georgian city, comprising the ancient cities of London (the City) and Westminster, and the districts of Bloomsbury, Mayfair, Marylebone, Holborn, Islington, Shoreditch, Bethnal Green, Bow and Southwark, very different in their social composition and physical appearance. It also had more clearly defined limits than later in the century, although it was already by the 1820s what William Cobbett, the radical writer, called, sarcastically, a 'great' or 'infernal' Wen.

The radical publisher G. W. M. Reynolds began his highly successful volumes *The Mysteries of London* in 1846 with a lurid prologue in which he referred both to London's 'boundless magnitude' and its 'fearful contrasts'. 'A thousand towers pointed upwards from horizon to horizon'. Yet 'the most unbounded wealth' was 'the neighbour of the most hideous poverty' and 'the most gorgeous pomp' was placed in relief by 'the most deplorable squalor'.

Within the great Wen, the London that mattered most was *north* of the Thames. The nation's financial centre, including the Bank of England and the Stock Exchange, was located in the City proper. North of the Thames, too, were the cultural, business and administrative centres – Whitehall, Parliament, the Courts and the Palace. However, there were important tracts of common land south of the river, including the commons at Kennington and further away at Clapham; and there was Lambeth Palace, the London home of the Archbishop of Canterbury.

There had been significant changes in London's economic and political life before 1849. In particular, its industries had already declined, while those of the Midlands and the north of England had increased in size and volume of output. The old silk industry of Spitalfields, for example, was by now a problem industry, distinguished for its 'demoralised condition'. Yet important industrial activities remained and indeed expanded in London – among them printing, engineering and the manufacture of consumer goods, like matches, clothing, ale and soap. And, if there was less of a sense of 'class' in London than there was in the industrial north, with its factories and furnaces, there were highly-organised

A panorama of the River Thames in 1845

London 'trades', groups of workers associated collectively, with the shoemakers largest in numbers and the tailors second.

Finally, given the rate of change in London, building was a major activity, and it too encouraged workers' association. Even before Queen Victoria came to the throne, there were many massive construction projects in London – streets, docks and, later, railways and tunnels. The great new system of underground sewers, an enormous engineering feat, had not begun to be built, however, when Marx arrived – London was deliberately excluded from the provisions of England's first national Public Health Act in 1848 – nor had work started on the Thames Embankment.

House building had its ups and downs, with a huge boom during the 1820s in the western districts adjacent to London, a development that reached and engulfed nearby villages like Paddington. One name, since lost, Tyburnia, derived from Tyburn Tree (now Marble Arch), was applied to an area which included Paddington, Bayswater, Notting Hill and North Kensington. Another area, Belgravia, was to spread out in the 1850s to Chelsea, Pimlico and to include Victoria (although the railway station named after the Queen was not opened until 1860).

Moving from one part of London to another, except on foot, was not easy – or

Building an underground sewer in Fleet Street

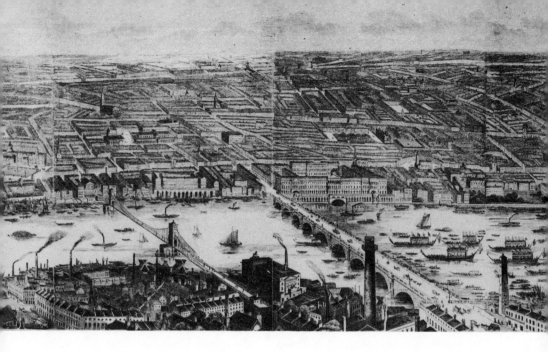

cheap – for many Londoners when Marx arrived. The first Underground station was not opened until 1863, and the horse bus, while commonplace, was still a relative novelty. The first two omnibuses, hauled by three horses, had been introduced in 1829 by George Shillibeer, a British-born coach-builder, who had lived in Paris. They plied between Paddington Green along the New Road – now Marylebone and Euston Road – and past the Angel, Islington, to the Bank of England; by 1849 there were 620 of them. It was already possible to travel from Charing Cross to Camden Town for one penny, and there were many threepenny fares. Yet it was not until 1856 with the foundation of the London General Omnibus Company that small operators, seeking custom on profitable routes, gave way to the large fleet owner offering a general service.

River transport persisted too, with steamers carrying 125 passengers plying backwards and forwards between London Bridge and Westminster all day from eight a.m. to nine p.m. Nonetheless, merchants and lawyers, as well as clerks, and most warehousemen and artisans, might still walk to work. Even the City of London retained its character as a place to live as well as work, although it was soon to become the 'ghost city' at nightfall when the thousands of office workers went back to the suburbs.

The railways were already arriving

A passenger on a London Knifeboard bus

Crowds arriving in London for the Great Exhibition in 1851

before Queen Victoria came to the throne, for in 1836 the Deptford line to London Bridge Station was complete. Euston Station was opened in 1837 and Waterloo Station in 1848 (Kings Cross was to follow in 1852). Railways did more to change the appearance and social life of cities than any other innovation, though their effects were complex and controversial. They led to huge investment – and employment – but also to wild speculation; to new warehouses and stations, but also to large-scale clearing of old houses; ultimately to more democratic modes of travel, but also to the creation of new social and physical divides, 'the two sides of the track'; to the large scale movement of goods, which made many of them cheaper, but to the spread of luxuries also; and, not least, to a new sense of time. Railways were associated both with regularity and punctuality (*Bradshaw*, the book of railway timetables first appeared in 1839) and, more disturbingly, with a speeding-up of life, and with inevitable accidents on the way.

Dickens's *Dombey & Son* (1848), has many memorable passages – as do his other works – about railways. He thought of them both as symbols of progress and as instruments of death.

The peak year of construction of new lines was 1846, and of miles of track completed 1848. The financial crash of 1847, which lay in the background of the European revolutions of 1848, was often attributed to railway speculation.

Migration to London, however, from other parts of the country, had long preceded the coming of the railway, and, in a decade of increased migration, Marx himself was only one of a large number of

London & Birmingham RAILWAY.

Acceleration of Trains.

The Public are informed that on and after

TUESDAY next, the 1st of AUGUST,

THE DOWN

DAY MAIL TRAIN,

Will depart from this Station

At 10 o'Clock

Instead of ¼ before 10 as at present.

It will consist exclusively of Four and Six Inside Mail Carriages, and will perform the entire Journey to Birmingham in Four Hours and a Half.

The same advantages and accommodation will be afforded to the Public by the

UpTrain leaving **Birmingham**

AT

¼ past 1 o'Clock,

P. M.

THE FARES BY THESE TRAINS WILL BE

First Class - - - - - - **32**s. **6**d.

Passengers with **Private Carriages,** and **Servants** in attendance on their Masters, **22**s. **6**d.

But Private Carriages cannot be conveyed by the Down Day Mail Train.

By Order,

Office, Euston Station,
26th July, 1843.

R. CREED,
Secretary

The imposing entrance to Euston Station, 1839

immigrants from both inside and outside Britain. Indeed, in the ten years between the Census of 1841 and 1851 some 330,000 newcomers arrived in London. There were sharp contrasts of experience and fortune among them. A few were to become rich through trade or connections. Large numbers, however, were to become artisans or domestic servants, whose 'upstairs–downstairs' contrasts persisted until after the end of the reign of Queen Victoria. Some immigrants moved downwards rather than upwards. No fewer than 120,000 people were evicted from their old homes between 1853 and 1900 as the railways and then the Underground were extended. Nor were the poor ever eliminated, though they might often be moved from one place to another: 'The poor', *The Times* wrote in 1861, 'are displaced, but not removed'.

Already during the 1840s there was a sharp contrast in building densities in different parts of London – the word 'overcrowding' was first used in the 1840s, moreover social statisticians were interested in relating such differences to other social indicators like those of sickness and crime. There was a network of private schools, and schools managed by religious denominations, but no general educational system until after 1870.

Meanwhile, public health arrangements, like housing, remained unsatisfactory. In the words of a recent historian, London was 'like a polluted sponge, a honeycomb of cesspools and wells, water supply taken from the rivers which were used as drains, perpetual fever haunting the slums, and thousands dying in successive epidemics of cholera.' The first 'visitation' of cholera to London had been in 1831 and there was a further epidemic in 1849, the year Marx arrived. Yet even more serious in their effects than cholera were less dramatic diseases like typhus. There was no accident in the fact that the highest London death rates were in Holborn, Shoreditch and Bethnal Green, the older, poorer districts. Nor was it any consolation that London was appreciably healthier than most European cities, and that the 'sanitary idea' had more disciples in London than socialism.

It was not until six years after Marx arrived that the Metropolitan Board of Works was created in 1855. It set about at once to devise 'a system of sewerage which should prevent all or any part of the sewage within the Metropolis from passing into

'A Court for King Cholera' a *Punch* cartoon of 1852 showing the insanitary conditions of London slums

the Thames in or near the Metropolis', and later on turned its attention to the widening of old streets and the making of new ones, the building of embankments to contain the Thames and the inspection of the gas supply. Slum clearance was more a by-product of these sanitary and environmental improvements and projects than a priority, but its effects were to be socially striking. London became more socially segregated, with its purpose-built single class streets that became characteristic of late-Victorian London.

The suburb which grew fastest in the late Victorian years was Camberwell: indeed, its population increased seven times between 1837 and 1901. It was a suburb for the respectable, among them, the growing numbers of clerks who formed an increasingly important element in the changing labour force. Already in the

1840s it had many fine houses, but in the next decades housing standards were to become more limited and uniform, until ultimately Camberwell became a place of standard two-storey brick terraces.

In the late-nineteenth century, London was to play an important part in the history of British socialism. During the late 1830s and early 1840s, however, it seemed in this respect to be lagging behind the industrial north, particularly during the early years of Chartism. Following the publication of the Charter in May 1838, it was largely the provincial Chartists who organised the world's first large scale working-class movement to secure their still famous 'six points' – votes for all; secret voting; annual parliaments; paid MPs; an end to the then necessary property-owning qualification for MPs; and the abolition of corrupt constituencies.

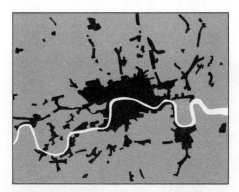

London at the end of the eighteenth century

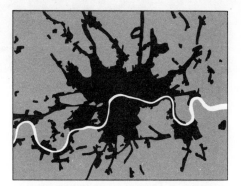

London in the 1830s

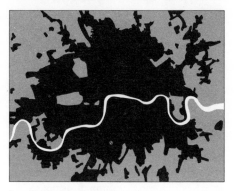

London in the 1870s

The expansion of London during the nineteenth century

'The worst mistake the Chartist leaders made,' wrote H. M. Hyndman, the socialist leader (who was influenced by Marx), 'was that they neglected London until too late.' Hyndman's statement was exaggerated in relation to the whole history of Chartism, for although London was relatively inactive at the beginning of the Chartist story in 1838–9, it was always a major centre of active working-class politics.

The National Union of the Working Classes had been founded in London in 1831, and there were meetings and demonstrations, like a huge Coldbath Fields gathering in 1833. Around Lincoln's Inn and the Temple there was a collection of radical bookshops, well supported by the public, with the unstamped *Poor Man's Guardian* defying the newspaper tax.

The London Working Men's Association was founded in June 1836 by the leaders of the 'intelligent and influential portion' of the working classes and the more militant East London Democratic Association in 1837. Yet it was not until 1848 that London was at the centre of the Chartist story. There were active revolutionary elements in the London Chartism of that year, when different London labour groups, including workers in the 'old trades', rallied to the movement, and some of the most active Chartists turned increasingly to socialist programmes. Nor did Chartist sentiment evaporate after 1848. 'The artisans', wrote Henry Mayhew, author of *London Labour & the London Poor* (1851), 'are almost to a man, red-hot proletarians, entertaining violent political opinions.'

There were four elements in the London situation which had held back revolutionary forces in 1848 itself – at a time when revolution was sweeping

The 1842 Chartist petition being presented to the House of Commons

Europe. First, the propertied London middle classes were strong and in critical situations rallied to the cause of law and order. Second, many radicals were not revolutionaries. They were, for various reasons, unwilling to use physical force. Third, London workers were better paid than workers in the provinces, a fact of great importance in 1838, when the Chartists were stronger in the capital than they were outside, and significant even ten years later when there was obvious distress in the capital and serious unemployment. Fourth, the well-organised Metropolitan police provided a readily available non-military form of control. The force had been founded in 1829 and was able to penetrate the movement through spies and informers.

When the Chartists demonstrated in 1848 at the famous Kennington Common meeting, south of the river, on 10 April, hoping to present a petition to Parliament, the forces of law and order were well prepared, and the Duke of Wellington,

hero of the Battle of Waterloo, was able to direct them efficiently. Their strongest forces were positioned at Blackfriars Bridge, the Chartists' proposed point for crossing the Thames. Four hundred Metropolitan Police were there, forty of them on horseback.

Earlier assembly points for organised labour in London had been closer to the working-class districts of London: Copenhagen Fields in Islington, for example, but this had largely been built up by 1848, while Hyde Park and Trafalgar Square were too far away for most demonstrators and the disturbances there belong to a later generation.

The revolutionary danger in London *after* Kennington Common came not from open assemblies but from secret groupings. Marx did not arrive in the city on the eve of revolution. For while it had known great excitements in 1848, thereafter it saw even its reform movements divide, collapse or peter out rather than be suppressed by force. Marx was to stay in London for the

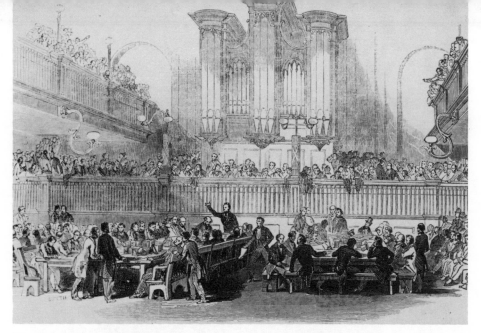

The Chartist Convention, London, 1848

Mass demonstration of Chartists on Kennington Common in 1848. (A rare daguerreotype)

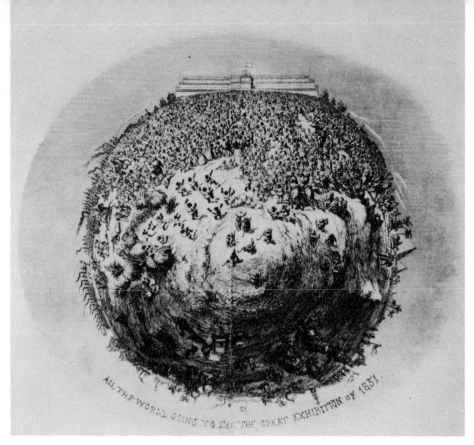

The Great Exhibition of 1851: a contemporary view

remaining thirty-four years of his life, after 1850 more conscious for most of the time, perhaps, of the wealth and power of London than of its revolutionary potential. There was a renewal of prosperity after the financial crisis of 1847 and the unemployment and hunger of 1848, and Engels himself wrote later that by the end of 1850 'anyone who had eyes to see – and was prepared to use them – was bound to appreciate that the storms of revolution were subsiding'.

Within three years of Kennington Common, immense crowds were to mass in London, not for political demonstration, but quietly to look round the great International Exhibition, in the newly-built Crystal Palace in Hyde Park. There was more pride in industrial achievement than fear of social breakdown.

3
Exiles And Revolutionaries

The London of the 1840s, like Paris, included a significant exile and revolutionary population both before and after the revolutions of 1848. If Paris since 1789 had been considered the natural centre of European revolution, so that the Russian exile Alexander Herzen, in his own words, 'entered it with reverence' in 1847, 'as men used to enter Jerusalem and Rome', London was known to be a place of sanctuary. Exiles and revolutionaries could find a greater freedom there not only after 1851, when France became a Napoleonic Empire again, but on the eve of the revolutions of 1848, when Louis Philippe was still in control.

Even between these dates, there were so many shifts of fortune in the French Revolution – and its attitude towards exiles and revolutionaries – that the security of London was prized. In 1834, indeed, the French Utopian socialist Étienne Cabet had used the British Museum in London as a base when he wrote his *Voyage en Icarie*. A third capital city, Brussels, had some of the advantages both of London and of Paris, but it was never a place for a long-term stay. Nor was Switzerland, though it too retained its appeal for revolutionary exiles through into the twentieth century.

Baron Bunsen, the Prussian Ambassador in London, reported in 1851 that there were then about a thousand foreign refugees who belonged to political associations of one kind and another. The numbers had increased since 1849, when Marx arrived in London to stay, but there were already two hundred and fifty members of the German Workers' Education Society in London as early as 1846 when Karl Schapper, its organiser, wrote to Marx about the Society's activities. They were concentrated in the London that Marx came to know well – with a rented hall in Drury Lane. Yet

Alexander Herzen, the Russian exile

The Red Lion public house in Soho's Great Windmill Street: above it is the room where the German Workers' Education Society met

Schapper eagerly reported also that the Society was 'trying to get into Whitechapel, where there are thousands of Germans' and where a branch had at last been founded.

The German Workers' Education Society, founded in 1840 in **Great Windmill Street** (see map on p 43) on the edge of Soho and not far from Piccadilly Circus, believed that 'all men were brothers' and in 1847 it included in its ranks – according to Schapper – forty Scandinavians, twenty Hungarians, 'and in addition Poles, Russians, Italians, Swiss, Belgians, French, English, etc'.

Broadly speaking, there were more or less distinct and coherent national groups among the exiles and revolutionaries in London, with nationalism a lively and influential ideology amongst them, particularly among the Poles, whose nation had been suppressed, and among the Italians, whose nation had still not been united. Schapper left the Italians out of his list: they were, indeed, for the most part strongly opposed to socialism. Giuseppe Mazzini's 'Young Italy' movement was liberal, and relied, though not exclusively, on strong middle-class support.

The claims of different nations and of humanity as a whole were taken to be complementary, however, so that there was always a great deal of international activity – not least on national anniversary days. Moreover, since the forces of order against which the exiles were in revolt were thought, often correctly, to be in alliance with each other across the borders of states (some of which, like the Hapsburg Empire, were multi- and anti-national), it seemed to be a duty of the exiles and revolutionaries as a whole to work against common enemies. This was true, indeed, both before the revolutionary uprisings of 1848 began and after 1849, when the European counter-revolution was consolidated. The

The 1848 revolutionary uprising in Paris. The mob burning the Emperor's throne in the Place Vendôme

part played by Russian armies in the process of consolidation increased hostility towards the Russian Empire so that Russian exiles and revolutionaries, who themselves had fled from Tsarist autocracy, were usually the least welcome groups in the exile and revolutionary groups.

The Poles by contrast were conspicuous in agitation and organisation from the start and received a warm welcome from the English Chartists, notably George Julian Harney, who met Engels in 1843 at the office of the Chartist newspaper *The Northern Star* in Leeds (its London office was in Great Windmill Street) and commissioned from him two long articles on European socialism.

William Lovett, one of the founders of the London Working Men's Association and a very different kind of 'moral force' Chartist, was just as internationalist in outlook as Harney and in 1844 formed the first international society in London, the Democratic Friends of All Nations. He had become a close friend of Giuseppe Mazzini and supported him strongly after the British Government had intercepted Mazzini's mail earlier that year. His new society, however, was not a success. It was not sufficiently militant to appeal to most exiles, and a far more successful organisation, the Fraternal Democrats, was launched by Harney in September 1845 at a banquet held to celebrate the French Republican constitution of 1792. It included Frenchmen, Germans, Poles, who had their own democratic society, Swiss, Hungarians and even one 'Turkish democrat', who sang Turkish songs to the assembled guests at the founding banquet.

Not all exiles and revolutionaries in London were convinced, however, by Harney's left-wing Chartism: indeed, social differences between exiles and revolutionaries usually counted for more

William Lovett, a prominent Chartist

Giuseppe Mazzini, the Italian revolutionary

than national differences then and later, and there were bitter divisions amongst the London Poles following the Cracow uprising in 1846. Yet the German groups, in particular, moved further to the left between 1847 and 1849 and were ready to welcome Marx. By occupation most of them were artisans. Schapper was a compositor, Moll a watchmaker, Bauer a shoemaker. A fourth activist who was to play an important part in the future Marxist story, was Johann Georg Eccarius, a tailor.

Karl Schapper, who became German secretary of the Fraternal Democrats, had been an exile in Paris before he came to London, and had participated, like Joseph Moll and Heinrich Bauer, in the abortive Paris insurrection of 1839. They were all members of a secret society, the League of the Just, *Bund der Gerechten*, founded in 1836, and were already seasoned 'professional revolutionaries'. Schapper had participated, for example, in an attack on a Frankfurt guardhouse in 1833 and had joined an abortive Mazzini expedition to Savoy in 1836.

The German Workers' Education Society provided a cover for the activities of the League of the Just, but it had a vigorous social and cultural life of its own – and an offshoot, the Sunday Club, which attracted even the non-politically minded. In his letter to Marx in 1846, Schapper not only outlined the way the Education Society worked, but caught its style and mood:

'Our Society numbers about 250 members. We meet three times a week. On Tuesdays there are alternately reports on current politics and discussions: one Tuesday is devoted to Feuerbach's *Religion of the Future*, which we are discussing paragraph by paragraph, and the next to questions raised by members of the Society themselves. The latest question which we discussed was the upbringing of youth in a Communist State. Our problem is to give all members of the Society an opportunity to raise for discussion any question concerning our principles which is not yet clear to them, in this way seeking complete clarity. Saturday evening is devoted to singing, music, recitations and reading interesting newspaper articles; on Sunday lectures are given on ancient and modern history, geography, astronomy, etc, and then questions of the present position of the workers and their attitude to the bourgeoisie are discussed in turn . . . On Mondays the French Society meets, at which the system of Communism is discussed. True, it still looks very like Republicanism, but nevertheless we learn something there, and have the opportunity to acquaint the Frenchmen with our ideas.

'Once a fortnight we meet jointly with the English (the "Fraternal Democrats"), and I can say that these meetings have already been very valuable for both sides . . .

'On Wednesday evenings there are singing lessons, on Thursdays language and drawing lessons, on Fridays dancing lessons. Our library numbers about 500 books: in addition, we have geographical and astronomical globes, maps, and German, French, English and Scandinavian newspapers. We keep up good connections in France, Switzerland, Scandinavia, Hungary, Germany, America and other countries where there are former members of our Society; they inform us from time to time of the successes of the movement in their countries.'

Schapper's letter was sent to Marx in Marx's capacity as organiser of the Communist Correspondence Committee, set up in Brussels, where Marx and Engels were in exile, in 1845. They had already reached the conclusion stated clearly by Marx in 1845 (in his theses on Ludwig Feuerbach, the German materialist philosopher), that 'the philosophers have only *interpreted* the world in various ways. The *point however is to change it*'. They also visited England together during the summer of 1845, when Engels took Marx to Manchester to show him not only what

The Gothic splendour of Chetham's Library in Manchester where both Marx and Engels studied in the 1840s and after

Europe's major industrial city was like but the famous Chetham's Library, which included a sizeable collection of works by British economists.

Before examining the pattern of Marx's contacts with the exile and revolutionary groups in London before and after his arrival to stay in the city in 1849, it is necessary to describe his social, political and intellectual background more fully – how he came to be in Brussels, what were his associations with Paris, and why he wanted to turn to the British economists to help him understand the nature of society and the prospect of revolution.

4
The Marxes

Marx was one of nine children, although only four of them survived into adult life, and he was the only boy to do so. Both his parents came from an orthodox Jewish background, but his father, Heinrich, had taken full advantage of the greater freedom allowed to Jews during French rule in Trier from 1803 to 1818 to rise to a highly-respected position as a lawyer by the time Karl was born. He turned his back on his Jewish heritage, however, after the French left and was baptised a Lutheran. This meant that Karl himself was outside the Jewish community. Moreover, the Lutherans were themselves a minority in Catholic Trier.

Karl was quite fond of his older sister, Sophie, but does not seem to have been close to his mother, Henrietta, particularly later in life. Through his mother's family, however, he was to have an intriguing connection with the modern capitalist world. His uncle, B. F. D. Philips – from whom Karl would try, throughout his life, usually without success, to borrow money – was a banker at Zaltbommel in Holland. Marx would regularly visit him on his way to Trier, when he would meet his cousins, Gerard and Anton Philips, who were to go on – in 1891 – to found what has now become Philips Electrical Industries in Eindhoven. When descendants of the two families met on one occasion, it is said that the Philips branch remarked to the Marx branch 'You talked about capital, whilst we made it . . .'

Karl had a warm, affectionate relationship with his father, who was a well-educated man with a keen interest in French rationalist philosophy. Another

10 Bruckenstrasse: the house where Marx was born in Trier

formative influence in his teenage years
was a great friend of the family, Baron von
Westphalen, a liberal, intelligent man with
a strong leaning towards romanticism. It
was von Westphalen who encouraged Karl
to read, lent him books and spent much
time talking with him.

At the age of seventeen, after graduating
from his secondary school eighth in a
class of thirty-two, Karl entered Bonn
University as a student of Law, where he
threw himself into student life, forgetting
to write home, writing instead Byronic
poems, accumulating debts, sometimes
getting drunk. The up-shot was that after
one year at Bonn, his father decided he
should transfer to Berlin University, where
he hoped there would be a more sober,
studious atmosphere. There was, however,
a problem. Before starting his studies at
Berlin, Karl had fallen in love with Baron

An impression of Karl Marx as a young man

Humboldt University in Berlin as Marx would have found it

Jenny von Westphalen, Karl Marx's future wife

von Westphalen's daughter, Jenny, a beautiful and charming auburn-haired, green-eyed girl, who had many suitors in Trier. She was twenty-two, but Karl was only eighteen, and there was a more marked difference still in their social status, since Jenny's grandmother was a Scottish noblewoman descended from the the the Dukes of Argyll. Nonetheless, Karl and Jenny overcame family opposition on both sides and their engagement was approved before Karl left the Rhineland and his fiancée and travelled to Berlin.

Berlin before the revolutions of 1848 was a capital city with 400,000 inhabitants. It had a tense feeling about it, perhaps because whilst being the seat of Prussian bureaucratic rule, it was a magnet for German radical intellectuals. The great German philosopher Hegel had taught there from 1818 to 1831, and some of his pupils had drawn radical conclusions from what he had written. Karl felt the excitement, particularly in the Doctors' Club, where 'Young Hegelian' ideas of a radical kind were freely discussed, and to the dismay of his father, who had wished him to study Law, found himself increasingly drawn towards the study of philosophy. He gradually established a reputation among the radical intellectuals for his wit, erudition and firm stance on philosophical issues, and in 1841 graduated as a Doctor of Philosophy; his thesis on Ancient Greek philosophy had contemporary significance and he had high hopes of an academic career.

When this did not materialise, he turned to journalism as a means of earning his living, and moved back to the Rhineland, where he began to contribute to *Rheinische Zeitung*, a progressive journal, published in Cologne. Within ten months, in October 1842, he was made editor. His leaders and articles were radical and uncompromising, but somehow they evaded the censor, until the circulation rose and the Prussian Government were forced to take notice of its polemic. Finally, after a particularly bitter attack on the Russian Tsar, the newspaper was suppressed in March 1843.

Karl was still only twenty-four, but he decided that if he wanted to write about the things in which he believed he would have to leave Germany. Before doing so, however, he married Jenny at the Evangelical Church in Trier in June 1843. The length of their engagement had not taken the edge off their relationship: neither did the hardships of the years to come destroy it. They honeymooned in Switzerland and set up home in Paris, which had been suggested as a destination by Arnold Ruge, leader of the Young Hegelians. On their arrival in Paris in

October of 1843 the Marxes lodged at 23 rue Vaneau. By then, Jenny was four months pregnant with their first child, also to be called Jenny.

first-born – were to stay in the rue Vaneau until leaving for Brussels in February 1845.

Karl spent long nights in Paris avidly reading books on economics, politics and

The great German philosopher, Georg Hegel, lecturing at Berlin University

The rue Vaneau was in St Germain on the Left Bank, close to the government offices along the Quai D'Orsay, and there were many other German emigrants living in the area. Here they set up a primitive attempt at a commune with the families of Ruge – with whom Marx was collaborating as joint editor of the *Deutsche-Französiche Jahrbücher* – and Germain Mauer – another German socialist émigré. The arrangement did not please the newly-married Jenny and within a fortnight, they had moved out, eventually to settle at number 38 rue Vaneau. The façade of the house still stands today, but with a rich irony that applies to so many of the revolutionaries' haunts, the interior has been converted to a block of exclusive luxury flats, selling, in 1982, for nearly £200,000. Marx and Jenny – plus their

philosophy and writing manuscripts which were not to be published until almost half a century after his death. Above all, he read as much as he could on the French Revolution of 1789, seeking to discover why it had 'failed' and how it could be continued. He was made welcome in Paris 'salons', where he met writers and artists, the Russian revolutionary Bakunin, and the German romantic poet, Heine.

Yet the hope of France, Karl came to argue, did not depend on the talkers in the salons, but on the proletariat in the streets, manual workers who were, he argued, exploited by their masters. Politics had an economic and social base for 'the course of world history was determined by definite laws and in any society the social and political stature of the state was determined by the way in which goods were produced'.

Below left: the German poet, Heinrich Heine

Below right: the Russian anarchist, Michael Bakunin

Opposite: Paris: the Napoleon Column in the Place Vendôme

'Communists' – and Karl did not hesitate to use the word – should be 'the first to stress social questions.' Given these convictions, therefore, he came into contact with the League of the Just, persuading the leaders to alter its programme so that within a few years it was a socialist body, later to be renamed the Communist League. At the same time, he was supporting himself and Jenny by writing articles for journals published in Paris for German distribution such as *Vorwärts* and the *Deutsche-Franzözische Jahrbücher*, of which only one issue was ever produced.

It was through such journalism that he was drawn into close association with Engels, who was to become his life-long friend, collaborator and, on many occasions, financial supporter. The two men had first met in Cologne in November 1842, but it was not until Engels wrote an article '*Outline of a Critique of Political Economy*' for the *Jahrbücher* that the two men realised

in Paris during the summer of 1844 how much they had in common. They were to go on to collaborate in writing *The Holy Family* in 1845 (an attack, mainly written by Marx, on some of the leading 'young Hegelians') and *The German Ideology*, written in the spring of 1846. By then the Prussians had successfully put pressure on the French government of Louis Philippe to suppress the German journals published in Paris, and Marx and other revolutionaries were expelled from France in February 1845, moving on to Brussels, where industrialisation was more advanced than in France and where there was considerable socialist ferment. Two children were born to them there – Laura in 1846 and Edgar in 1847. They were forced to move lodgings many times and, as a foretaste of the future, had to borrow money and to pawn their belongings in order to live.

Engels joined the Marxes in the spring of 1845, and in the summer they were

living next door to each other at numbers 5 and 7 rue de l'Alliance. They spent their time arguing with other socialists and in the process clarifying their own thinking as

Edgar Marx, Karl Marx's son born in 1847

they wrote *The German Ideology*. It did not find a publisher. They were drawn increasingly into a web of revolutionary activity through the Communist Correspondence Committee which they set up in 1846. The German Workers' Association in Brussels was part of the network, and so, too, from June 1846 was the German Workers' Education Society in London.

Short visits to London, first by Engels in June 1847, and later by Marx and Engels in November 1847, involved what Engels called 'decisive' discussions with the Communist League. In addition, they attended a meeting of the Fraternal Democrats on 29 November, the anniversary of the Polish rising of 1830, and they addressed a meeting of the German Workers' Education Society. The slogan of the Communist League, which claimed a membership of five hundred, had been changed at the insistence of

Engels from 'All men are brothers' to 'Workers of all countries unite' in line with their increasingly sharp assault on all older or rival versions of 'utopian socialism'. There were a lot of men, Marx observed, whose brother he did not wish to be. Their by now well-articulated philosophy of action rested not on 'sentiment' but upon a 'scientific' conclusion that 'the capitalist mode of production' would 'inevitably' collapse: indeed, the collapse was 'daily taking place before our eyes'.

At the behest of the Communist League, which was in touch with Paris, Brussels, Switzerland and Sweden, Marx produced the *Communist Manifesto* of 1848, which appeared in German in February 1848 on the eve of Europe's great chain of revolutions. It was a tract for the times, but in very different times it was to remain a landmark document to be used by future revolutionaries throughout the world. Its appeal lay not only in its dazzling language, but in its content. It ranged widely over the past, summarised the present, and peered into the future, claiming boldly that revolution was bound to come. The prosperity and power of the middle class, who had achieved unprecedented control over production forces, were doomed to disappear. It had forged the weapons that

Neue Rheinische Zeitung.
Organ der Demokratie.

№ 1.   Köln, Donnerstag, 1. Juni   1848.

[Masthead newspaper facsimile in Fraktur — subscription and editorial notices, including the Redaktions-Comité:]

Redaktions-Comité.

Karl Marx, Redakteur en Chef.

Heinrich Bürgers,
Ernst Dronke,
Friedrich Engels,
Georg Weerth,
Ferdinand Wolff,   } Redakteure.

---

bring 'death to itself' – the new proletariat – which had become a revolutionary class with nothing to lose but its chains.

There was, of course, no revolution in England in 1848 for reasons which Marx and Engels did not explore, and the *Manifesto* made very little impact in Britain, even though it was translated into English two years later, in the *Red Republican*, a new periodical edited by the Chartist, Harney. By then, however, revolutionary Europe had given way to reaction. Karl's own story was as complicated as the international pattern of events. He had been expelled from Brussels on 4 March 1848 with so little notice that Jenny had to leave her silver plate and best linen behind, and after a month in revolutionary Paris (from which he saw the Communist League disintegrate) he and Jenny had moved to Cologne where Karl edited the *Neue Rheinische Zeitung*. He survived a number of writs against him before his newspaper, which was advocating an armed uprising, was suspended in September. Although it resumed publication in October, he found it difficult to find the necessary funds and he was concerned about the counter-revolutionary course of events both in Germany and in France. Finally, on 16 May 1849, he was served with notice of expulsion. (His newspaper lasted for three more days, the final number appearing in red ink.)

From there he moved to other parts of Germany (at Frankfurt Jenny had to pawn still more of her family silver) before finding temporary refuge in Paris. Karl arrived in London in the late summer, three months before Engels, spending his first nights in Camberwell. His earlier visits had been brief. This time, he was to stay in England, which had escaped the reaction as well as the revolution, for the rest of his life; his wife and three children followed three weeks later.

The Marx's first family home in London was in one of the fashionable parts of the city – even then – **4 Anderson Street** (see map on page 36), just off the King's Road in Chelsea. It was there that a fourth child, Henry, was born, in the fourth country of Marx's long exile, on Guy Fawkes Night, 1849. Life in Chelsea proved comfortable, and, after so many adventures, to Jenny's liking, at least for a while. Yet the rent, £6 a month, was high in those days, and not surprisingly, with no money coming in, the Marxes very quickly got into debt. After the local tradesmen had pressed for payment of their bills, the bailiffs were called in and seized everything that could be taken, including the baby's cradle and the girls' toys. The whole family was evicted unceremoniously, to the delight of a watching crowd.

As Jenny described life with the baby at the time; 'you will see that few emigrants, perhaps, have gone through anything like it. As wet-nurses here are too expensive I decided to feed my child myself in spite of continual terrible pains in the breast and back. But the poor little angel drank in so much worry and hushed-up anxiety that he was always poorly and suffered horribly day and night. Since he came into the world he has not slept a single night, two or three hours at the most and that rarely.'

The Marxes' first family home in London, 4 Anderson Street situated in fashionable Chelsea

MARX FAMILY TREE

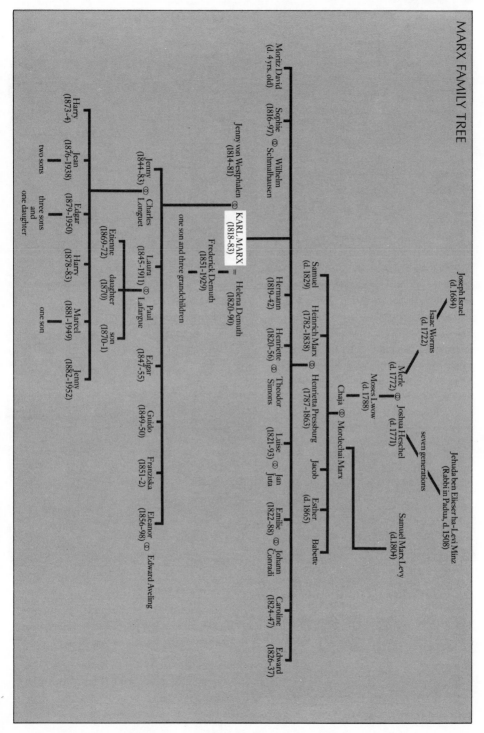

As for the eviction, 'there were two or three hundred persons loitering around our door – the whole Chelsea mob. The beds were brought in again – they could not be delivered to the buyer until after sunrise next day. When we had sold all our possessions we were in a position to pay what we owed to the last farthing. I went with my little darlings to the two small rooms we are now occupying in the **German hotel** (see map opposite), 1 Leicester St., Leicester Square. There for £5 per week we were given a humane reception.'

The German Hotel was a transit camp for the many political refugees who had fled from the failed revolutionary upheavals in France, Italy, Austria and Germany: it is now a fish restaurant called Manzi's. The Marxes did not stay there long either. They had to find £5 a week for their accommodation, and in Jenny's simple words, 'one morning our host refused to serve us our breakfast and we were forced to look for other lodgings'.

ANDERSON STREET

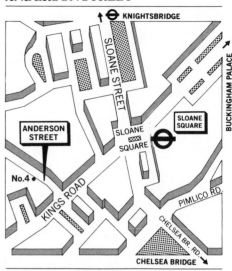

LEICESTER STREET

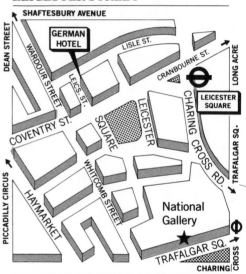

The German Hotel today

How to get there:

Anderson Street, SW3: by underground to Sloane Square Station (District and Circle lines) by bus – routes: **11, 19, 22, 137**

Leicester Street, WC2: by underground to Leicester Square Station (Piccadilly and Northern lines)
by bus – routes: **1, 24, 29, 176**

5
Soho Years

The first real home in Soho for the family was not far from the German Hotel – **64 Dean Street** (see map on page 43).

'We found two rooms in the house of a Jewish lace dealer', wrote Jenny, 'and spent a miserable summer there with the four children.' The original house no longer exists, and they stayed there only from 8 May to 2 December 1850.

Their home for the next six years was to be two rooms in the same street, in the top floor of number 28. Today the house bears a blue memorial plaque affixed by the Greater London Council, with the incorrect inscription, 'Karl Marx, 1818–1883, lived here 1851—1856' (in fact it should read 1850–1856). This is the only place where Marx's thirty-four years in England are thus commemorated.

When the family moved into number 28 in January or February 1851, Jenny was pregnant again, and a fifth child, Franziska, was born in March, scarcely before they were settled in their cramped apartment. Their landlord was an Italian-born cook, John Marengo. They also had living with them their faithful maid 'Lenchen', whose real name was Helene Demuth, together with an English nurse for Jenny's confinement. Shortly after their arrival Karl was recorded by the Census Enumerator of 1851 as 'Charles

Mark, Doctor (Philosophical Author)'.

Cosmopolitan Soho was already a favourite district for French, Italians, Swiss, Germans and others. Many of them were employed in the catering business, and even today Marx's house is part of a well-known restaurant of Italian origin, Leoni's. The other occupants in 1851, the year of the Great Exhibition, were an Italian-born confectioner and a 'teacher of languages', Morgan Kavanagh, who sub-let his part of the house to Marx.

The commemorative GLC Blue Plaque on 28 Dean Street (complete with incorrect dates)

Number 28 is a typical narrow-fronted Georgian house, simple but elegant, dating from 1734. There are many such houses in London, and, although the Victorians were reacting against the formal Georgian style,

Helene Delmuth, the faithful 'Lenchen'

28 Dean Street, as it was in the nineteenth century

they were remarkably flexible in their patterns of use. They could easily be adapted for other uses beside private residence, and they could be turned into hotels, offices and shops. The houses of Dean Street and some of the neighbouring streets were among the most beautiful in London, but they lacked most of the conveniences of a later generation. There would have been a primitive water closet at that time, albeit a communal one on the ground floor and not flushed from the mains water supply. Water came into the house in iron pipes so that the family was spared the indignity of having to go to the nearest public pump for fresh water, but the pressure would only bring it up to a height of ten feet above ground. Life must have been hard for Lenchen, who had to fetch the water for the washing and cooking and laundry from the ground floor.

Much of old Soho remains today and it is a district of narrow byways with

a crowded outdoor market in Berwick Street. The important 'boundary streets' were built much later, however – Shaftesbury Avenue (1877–1886) and Charing Cross Road (1887), and these sliced through some of the worst slums. The neighbourhood during the 1850s was noisy, bustling and cheerful, perhaps more so than today, when it is largely given over to food, drink, sex and the film industry. Indeed, traditionally occupied as it was by small craftsmen, many of them foreigners, it must have seemed very much like home, squalid though corners of it were, to countless political exiles over the years. Despite his own problems, Marx served on a relief committee to help penniless refugees.

The Marx family was very cramped because Karl needed one of the two rooms for his study. Having soon realised that there was no likelihood of imminent revolution, he busied himself here in his self-appointed life's task of not only

28 Dean Street, as it is today, a well-known restaurant

interpreting the world but changing it.

At first he had put his hopes in a new body, the Universal Society of Revolutionary Communists, founded in April 1850, but this soon collapsed, as did the Communist League itself; it had split after he and Engels could no longer control it. Thereafter, he was to concentrate on study – he had secured a ticket for the British Museum in June 1850 – and on holding court to visiting European revolutionaries and the occasional Prussian police agent. Karl gave his advice on revolutionary strategy to everyone whom he found interesting, including some visitors who requested it. Here too he wrote at his desk, seeking to order and systematise as well as to extend his knowledge of economics and politics. Before 1850 was over he had edited from a distance five numbers of the *Neue Rheinische Zeitung*.

A Prussian police agent has left a report, of their home life in Dean Street which carries the ring of truth: 'As father and husband, Marx, in spite of his wild and restless character, is the gentlest and mildest of men. Marx lives in one of the worst, therefore one of the cheapest, quarters of London. He occupies two rooms. The one looking out on the street is the parlour and the bedroom is at the back. In the whole apartment there is not one clean and solid piece of furniture. A seller of second-hand goods would be ashamed to give away such a remarkable collection of odds and ends.

'When you enter Marx's room smoke and tobacco fumes make your eyes water so much that for a moment you seem to be groping about in a cavern, but gradually, as you grow accustomed to the fog, you can make out certain objects which distinguish themselves from the surrounding haze. Everything is dirty, and covered with dust, so that to sit down becomes a thoroughly dangerous business. Here is a chair with only three legs, on another the children are playing at cooking – this chair happens to have four legs. This is the one which is offered to the visitor, but the children's cooking has not been wiped away; and if you sit down, you risk a pair of trousers.'

Karl's working routine was, to say the

One of the rooms in 28 Dean Street

least, flexible, as the same agent witnessed: 'In private life he is an extremely disorderly, cynical human being, and a bad host. He leads a real gypsy existence. Washing, grooming and changing his linen are things he does rarely, and he is often drunk. Though he is often idle for days on end, he will work day and night with tireless endurance when he has a great deal of work to do. He has no fixed times for going to sleep and waking up. He often stays up all night, and then lies down fully clothed on the sofa at midday and sleeps till evening, untroubled by the whole world coming and going through the room.'

Karl's only paid employment from 1851 to 1862 was the writing of a regular column on European events for the *New York Daily Tribune*, a popular newspaper with a large circulation. He had met its editor, Charles Dana, in Cologne, and at first, because his command of the English language was as yet imperfect, it was Engels who wrote many of the articles that bore Karl's name. Karl contributed also, to the *People's Paper*, a periodical produced by the Chartist Ernest Jones, who, unlike Harney, accepted the main tenets of Marx's political philosophy. He worked also on the *Eighteenth Brumaire of Louis Napoleon*, a study of class struggle and politics in France and on the preparation of the *Contribution to the Critique of Political Economy*, which was to appear in 1859, the product, as he put it, of 'many years of conscientious research'.

As the spy noted, Karl worked late, smoking many cigars and often slept much of the day on a sofa. Until Engels came to his aid, he was very poor, once pawning his overcoat twice in the same year, 1853. He had become keenly conscious of what he called 'the petty, paltry, bourgeois struggle', which he knew was wearing out his wife, and seriously entertained for a time the idea of emigrating to the New World, as so many German exiles from the revolutions of 1848 had done. Lacking money to pay the fare across the Atlantic, he did not know that assisted passages could be offered to political exiles by the British Government. In December 1845 he had given up his Prussian nationality and remained stateless for the rest of his life, although he was to apply for, and to be refused, British citizenship in 1874.

Then, as always, the family's support was assured by Engels, who had moved back to Manchester in November 1850 to work as a clerk in his father's cotton business at a salary of £200 a year. Engels would have preferred to keep a fine table and a cellar of good wine, but ensured instead that his friend Karl was saved from the harshest extremes of poverty. Karl had

Cotton factories in Industrial Manchester in Engels' time

helped him in 1848 and 1849: now and for long afterwards he reciprocated. His first gift was £2. Thereafter money often arrived in separate envelopes, each containing for security two halves of different notes. Sometimes, however, there were only postage stamps. Whenever Karl was not borrowing money for himself – and sometimes even when he was – he would lend to those of his comrades whose need was, he felt, even greater than his and there were several of them. The years in Dean Street were, indeed, shabby and sad for others besides himself.

Karl also learnt how to avoid too great a pressure from his creditors. Thus, when the family doctor pressed for payment of his bill, the whole Marx family retreated for ten weeks to the house of a friend, Peter Imandt, in Camberwell and afterwards Karl hid in Manchester, in Engels' house, for another three months. This was only one of several trips to Manchester, which gave him a glimpse of the world of

machinery and steam, of capitalist production in operation. Engels lived permanently in Manchester until 1869, and Karl's visits there often lasted several weeks.

252 Hyde Road, Manchester: where Engels lived with his mistress, Mary Burns. The house is now demolished

Jenny Marx with her daughter, Jenny

The Whitfield Tabernacle as it is today

Jenny made one lengthy visit to her birthplace, Trier, in 1856, in order to be present at her mother's death bed. She had visited Germany and Holland two years earlier, and received a number of legacies in 1855 which enabled her to take back from the pawn shop silver, linen and clothes, though one trip, to see Marx's Dutch uncle in Holland, for money, was fruitless.

Three of the Marx children died in Dean Street – Henry, not one year old; the baby girl, Franziska, and Edgar or 'Mouche' 'little fly' – who died of consumption aged eight. All the children had nicknames, as Karl himself did – 'the Moor'. Edgar's funeral at the Whitfield Street Tabernacle, just off Tottenham Court Road (which it fronts today, having been rebuilt after bombing during the Second World War) was a deeply distressing affair, when Karl had to be

forcibly restrained from throwing himself into his son's grave.

Poverty meant a loss of dignity, felt most by his wife, Jenny, who confided to friends in her letters how she would often lie awake at night, weeping. Her chief duty was as Karl's unpaid secretary and fair copyist (even though her own handwriting and command of English were far from perfect: it was she who prepared things for the printer, since Karl's handwriting was illegible).

The cleaning and the cooking was done, of course, by Lenchen, (her nickname was 'Nimm'), who figures in the only real scandal of Marx's life. It was a common enough scandal for Victorian middle-class life, and earlier days too. When she became pregnant about the same time as Jenny Marx, and gave birth to a male child in June 1851, registered in August as Henry Frederick Demuth, there can have been little doubt as to the identity of the father. She was described at this time as no beauty, but 'nice looking with rather pleasing features . . .'

Jenny recorded simply in her autobiography that in the early summer of 1851, 'an event occurred that I do not wish to relate here in detail, although it greatly contributed to an increase in our worries, both personal and others'.

The boy was packed off at once to foster parents, Engels accepted paternity, and the affair was hushed up. Only on his death bed did Engels tell Eleanor the truth. Embarrassing as it had been to Marx especially, the birth did not mean the end of the family relationship. Nor did Lenchen leave. Karl and Jenny remained close even throughout this extremely difficult period.

The youngest Marx child, Eleanor, was born in January 1855, a few months before Edgar died in Karl's arms. She was described by Liebknecht as 'a merry little thing, as round as a bell and like cream and roses', and she was soon the favourite of the family.

DEAN STREET

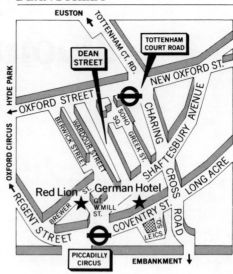

How to get there:

Dean Street, W1: by underground to Tottenham Court Road station (Northern and Central lines)
by bus – routes: 1, 7, 8, 14, 19, 22, 24, 25, 29, 38, 55, 73, 134, 176

6
Bloomsbury

From Dean Street Karl had to make only a short journey to work – to the Reading Room of the **British Museum** (see map on page 51) in Bloomsbury. He could walk up Dean Street to Soho Square and from there into Oxford Street, which was even then an important shopping centre. Although the modern department store had not yet reached London, Karl would have seen the large plate-glass windows that were installed during the 1840s in big, busy shops. Few early nineteenth-century dwelling houses remain in Oxford Street, and the short stretch of modern Tottenham Court Road would be very strange to him. But, there would have been more noise then than now – the noise of thousands of iron-rimmed carriage and cart wheels. In summer the air was thick with powdered horse dung, and in rainy

The entrance hall of the old British Museum, Montagu House, in 1845

The British Museum today

weather great heaps of filth would be brushed clear of the crossing places. Today, Marx would stride past a modern landmark: the YMCA building, along Great Russell Street, to the British Museum.

If any part of London could lay claim to be the 'intellectuals' quarter', it was Bloomsbury, although Carlyle once remarked caustically, 'there are several persons in a state of imbecility who come to read in the British Museum'. In the twentieth century it was to be associated with the name of the 'Bloomsbury Group', which included Virginia Woolf, Lytton Strachey and John Maynard Keynes and later with the massive, quintessentially 1930s, Senate building of London University. But the Bloomsbury Marx knew was the creation of the seventeenth and eighteenth centuries and of the development of the Bedford Estate.

Bloomsbury began with the restoration of the monarchy in 1660, when Bloomsbury Square was laid out and building started along a quiet country lane to the west of the square, to be known as Great Russell Street, from where Christopher Wren could look across open meadows to Highgate. One of those buildings in Great Russell Street was Montagu House. It had been a museum since 1759, when it began also to house the library of the Kings of England. The British Museum itself was created by Act of Parliament in 1753. Montagu House already provided reading rooms for scholars, but with the acquisition in 1823 of the vast library that had belonged to King George III, and a large private collection of pictures in the following year, the Trustees started work on a new building – a colossal project which took thirty-four years to complete.

From the time of the passing of the Copyright Act of 1842, a copy of every book, magazine, pamphlet or journal published in Britain had to be deposited with the British Museum (now the British Library). There are now thirty thousand new books added each year, with more than seven million volumes already on the

shelves. Even during the 1830s there was a growing demand for space for students to consult the books, and the energetic new Keeper of Printed Books, was the exiled Italian revolutionary, Antonio Panizzi (1797–1879), who ironically shared one link with Marx; Panizzi had fled the Duchy of Modena – 'beastly behind its beauty', Marx eventually went to live at Modena Villas, Kentish Town.

It was Panizzi who made a sketch of the sort of reading room he wanted and showed this to the designer of the Museum Building, Robert Smirke.

The result was one of the world's most famous – and useful – rooms, the great domed reading room perhaps the best-known section of the British

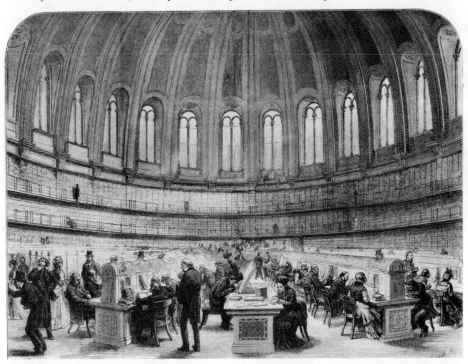

Museum, which by 1890 was receiving 900,000 visitors each year. The new library was opened in 1857 when Marx had already left Dean Street for the suburbs, and it is recorded that on opening day a champagne breakfast was laid out on the desks.

A year or two later, a French writer, Hippolyte Taine, left this impression 'The library contains 600,000 books: there is a huge Reading Room, circular and topped by a cupola, so arranged that no reader is far from the central bureau or has the light in his eyes. The surrounding shelves are filled with reference books, dictionaries, biographical collections, classics in every field, very well arranged and which one can consult on the spot. Moreover, on every table there is a small map or plan to show the order and position of these books. Each desk is isolated. You have nothing but the wood of your desk under your eyes and are not disturbed or bothered by the stares of a neighbour. The chairs are of leather and the desks are covered with leather too; all very neat and clean. Two pens to each desk, one quill and one steel. There is a small bookrest so that you can have a second book conveniently to hand or the book you are copying from. To get a book you write the title on a form which you hand in at the central bureau: a library clerk brings it to your own desk, and that very quickly; I tried this out and proved it, even with very rare books. You are responsible for the book until you have got

Karl Marx's reputed seat in the Reading Room

1868, while a later poet, W. B. Yeats, who spent many of his days at the British Museum, felt that he must have been very delicate, compared with such stalwarts, for he remembered 'putting off hour after hour consulting some necessary book because I shrank from lifting the heavy volumes of the catalogue.' On one occasion Shaw was observed consulting at the same time *Capital* and the orchestral score of Wagner's *Tristan & Isolde*. The only natural light in the Reading Room was from the glass dome, so when darkness came, usually about four o'clock on a winter's afternoon – or earlier on a foggy day (and the fogs of mid-Victorian London were notorious, as Dickens pointed out, in the memorable opening pages of *Bleak House*) reading became nearly impossible. In 1880 electric lighting was installed, but even that sometimes failed.

the form back. There is a special place for ladies which is most considerate.' The 'special place for ladies' has gone, but most of the account applies today.

Carlyle, Thackeray, Dickens, Mazzini, Ruskin all sat in this Reading Room, and Marx, one of the most diligent readers, was to be followed among hundreds more, by Gladstone, Shaw, Kropotkin, Gandhi and Chesterton. The poet Swinburne fainted there in the close atmosphere one day in

After obtaining his Reader's ticket in June 1850 – then as now a difficult task – Karl began by spending three months diligently reading back numbers of the *Economist*, followed by other periodicals and pamphlets. He ended his life by knowing more about the history of political economy in Britain than most professors of the subject.

During the mid 1860s when his health

And I declare that I am not under twenty-one years of age.

1832

I have read the "DIRECTIONS respecting the Reading Room,"
And I declare that I am not under twenty-one years of age.

1833   *Karl Marx, 1 Modena Villas, Maitland Park*,

I have read the "DIRECTIONS respecting the Reading Room,"
And I declare that I am not under twenty-one years of age.

Karl Marx's signature in the Reading Room's register of 16 March 1874

Karl Marx in 1861

deteriorated, and he was plagued by boils, Karl spent a lot of time reading text books on medicine, claiming to know more than any physician about the subject. He prescribed harsh cures for himself – including creosote, opium and arsenic, taken regularly for a long time.

It was in the old Reading Room that Karl worked on the *Address of the Central Committee to the Communist League* (1850), on *The Class Struggles in France* and the *Eighteenth Brumaire of Louis Bonaparte*. Of the last of these, Liebknecht wrote that the words in it were 'darts, spears . . . of a style that stigmatises, kills', but Karl was less happy about his many articles for the *New York Daily Tribune*. 'The continual newspaper muck annoys me', he complained. 'It takes a lot of time, disperses my effort and in the final analysis is nothing'.

In the new Reading Room – where legend has it that his seat was number 07 – Karl worked on a fascinating project which must have made the dispersal of effort particularly galling – his *Grundrisse*, which was not to become known in his lifetime, nor indeed in Lenin's, and, of course, on his most famous project of all, *Das Kapital*, volume one of which appeared in German in 1867. The *Grundrisse*, though it ranged widely over many economic and philosophical topics, was directly influenced by the financial crisis of 1857, which interrupted the relative prosperity of mid-Victorian England. *Das Kapital, A Critique of Political Economy*, is a remarkable book, the product of Marx the system builder; anxious to understand both the structure and the dynamics of capitalism throughout its history.

It is a massive book, beginning with economic theory and proceeding with history; yet the reader soon learns that the economic theory and the history are

intertwined throughout in a way that Marx himself thought of as providing 'scientific underpinning for independent working class action'. In writing it he drew, in his own words, not only on his own accumulated and critical knowledge but on 'hitherto unused *official* sources', the reports of official commissions of enquiry designed not to destroy capitalism but to strengthen it by controlling some of its social consequences.

The later volumes appeared after his death (Volume II in 1885, Volume III in 1894, twenty years after Volume I), and were edited by Engels from the notes that Marx left behind him. Volume IV, *Theories of Surplus Value*, was edited by Kautsky after Engels had died. The first English edition of Volume I did not appear for twenty years – long after a Russian translation, although Karl had hoped at

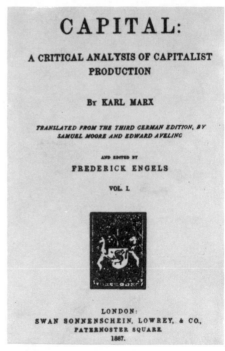

CAPITAL:

A CRITICAL ANALYSIS OF CAPITALIST PRODUCTION

By KARL MARX

TRANSLATED FROM THE THIRD GERMAN EDITION, BY SAMUEL MOORE AND EDWARD AVELING

AND EDITED BY
FREDERICK ENGELS

VOL. I.

LONDON:
SWAN SONNENSCHEIN, LOWREY, & CO.,
PATERNOSTER SQUARE.
1887.

The title page of the first English volume of *Das Kapital*, edited by Engels after Marx's death

once 'to find a publisher in England' to
improve his 'miserable material condition'.
The book received a number of favourable
reviews, in one of which, in the *Atheneaum*,
he was described as 'the prophet of the
working class'.

When *Das Kapital* was translated into
Russian, the Russian followers of Marx
were fearful lest the Tsarist censor should
ban the book, but they need not have
worried. The censors read it and found it
so hard to understand that they thought
few Russians would read it and fewer still
would comprehend what it was all about.

At least one Englishman,
H. M. Hyndman, the socialist leader who
read it in French, told Marx he 'learned
more from its perusal than from any other
book I ever read', while one of his fellow-
socialists actually learned French in order
to read it.

THE BRITISH MUSEUM

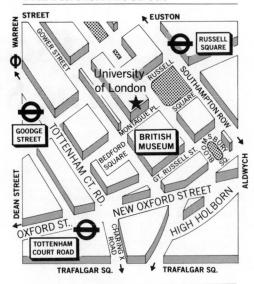

How to get there:

British Museum, Great Russell Street, WC1:
by underground to Tottenham Court Road
station (Northern and Central lines)
by bus – routes: 1, 7, 8, 14, 19, 22, 24, 25,
29, 38, 55, 73, 134, 176
Opening Times:
Monday–Saturday 10–5
Sundays 2.30–6
Closed: Good Friday, first Monday in
May, Christmas Eve, Christmas Day,
Boxing Day, New Year's Day

7
Escape
To The Suburbs

While Karl worked in the British Museum, Jenny stayed behind in Dean Street. In 1856 she inherited £150 from an uncle in Scotland; and shortly afterwards, on the death of her mother, she acquired a further inheritance – £120 – which in those days was quite enough to get the family out of what she called the 'evil, frightful rooms' in Dean Street and into 'a small house at the foot of romantic Hampstead Heath, not far from lovely Primrose Hill . . . When we slept in our own beds for the first time, sat on our own chairs and even had a parlour with second-hand furniture,' she wrote, 'then we really thought we were living in a magic castle.'

Number 9 **Grafton Terrace** (see map on page 58), Fitzroy Road, Kentish Town, remains much as it was when Jenny first saw it. A few years later, in the general 'tidying up' of addresses in expanding London, the name Fitzroy Road disappeared – to be found elsewhere in the district – and Grafton Terrace extended in length and changed its numbering. Number 9 became number 38, and then 46. It is a narrow three-storey 'town house' in a terrace, with a basement and a tiny back garden, and the front door is reached by a stone staircase from the pavement. The street itself remains unusually broad, and has a grand, spacious look. In 1856 it

was very new, having been built in 1849 on open fields.

Nearby Grafton Road is one of eight in London; there are in addition a Grafton Crescent and a Grafton Yard, close to each other, with another Grafton Crescent and a Grafton Place within two miles, and further away, a Grafton Mansions, a Grafton Street, Grafton Way, Grafton Square, Grafton Gardens and Grafton Close, all

elsewhere in London. The older Graftons are almost certainly named after Augustus Henry, third Duke of Grafton, who was Prime Minister from 1766–70. The country house of the Graftons in Suffolk was named Euston Hall.

Karl sometimes gave his address as Haverstock Hill, an important road linking Chalk Farm with Hampstead Village; though today, as then, Grafton Terrace is still on the 'wrong' side of that road, being very much part of the working-class district of Kentish Town, rather than the middle-class parts of Hampstead. Some working-class people had already moved out to Kentish Town by 1866: when a newspaper reporter asked a local inhabitant what had happened to people displaced by the building of a main line railway, he got the comprehensive reply:

'Some's gone down Whitechapel way, some's gone in the Dials ('Seven Dials' – a notorious slum in Central London); some's gone to Kentish Town, and some's gone to the Workhouse'.

There was a sense of openness about Kentish Town. When the Marxes moved there, it was described as 'throwing out lines of bricks and mortar to meet its neighbours, Hampstead Heath and Downshire Hill'. Once recommended by doctors as a salubrious place, it had been in social decline in the 1830s, but, paradoxically, it was saved by that great despoiler, the railway. The North London Railway had made little impact in the early fifties, even when it connected Hampstead and Kentish Town with Richmond in the south-west and Broad Street in the City. But in the 1860s, when the Midland Railway arrived, the map of Kentish Town was altered for ever, as streets were halted by great brick viaducts and the whole district was carved up into isolated sectors leaving a sizeable tract of land with no human habitation whatsoever. Yet the slums were

Number 46 Grafton Terrace today: the exterior and the living room and kitchen

Building the railway in London, Camden Town 1839

cleared and rents rose. Parts of the district were unmistakably middle-class.

Marx's house in Grafton Terrace, like so many of its kind, was rented. Because of the tendency of the building trade in London to over-production, there was usually an abundance of new houses at quite low rents for middle-class tenants and a glut of houses would bring rents well down. Thus, Karl paid only £36 a year in rent, in half-yearly instalments, for a house with a 'rateable value' of £24. Of his initial instalment of £4.20, £3.20 was for the Poor Rate, 10p for the sewers, 20p for lighting and water and a general rate for paving and other services. He always paid his rates on time.

Even when Karl died, only a quarter of London's houses had a constant water supply; most working-class tenants had only a single tap for the whole block; drainage was often faulty; and one water closet was usually shared by dozens of families. By contrast, the small house in

Grafton Terrace had two wcs.

For Karl, and for many others, Kentish Town was a thoroughly respectable middle-class address. For the first time since his family had been evicted from Anderson Street, they were now to dwell in decent surroundings amid respectable folk. But if Karl had attained middle-class status by moving to Grafton Terrace he had not altered the relationship to money that characterised his whole life. Long-suffering Engels, who had so often come to rescue in the Soho days, was called upon yet again therefore: 'Today I am actually worse off than I was five years ago when I was wallowing in the very quintessence of filth', wrote Karl in 1857, the year when England, too, was in financial crisis. A year later he borrowed £4 from Schapper and tried to raise sums from moneylenders also. 'The root of the trouble,' he claimed plaintively in that year, 'is that my modest income can never be used to pay for what I need *next* month. The money is absorbed by regular expenses such as rent, school fees, and payment of interest to the pawnbroker.'

There were other problems too. The house in Grafton Terrace had 'the four characteristics the English like in a house,' wrote Jenny. It was 'airy, sunny, dry and built on gravelly soil.' Yet, in spite of the dramatic view (on a clear day you could look down to St Paul's), there was as yet no proper road leading to the house and in the wet the mud was deep. Life in the suburbs was lonely too; Jenny had few friends, and the family – like most suburban families – was isolated, dependent on its own company. 'I often missed the long walks I had been in the habit of making in the crowded West End streets, the meetings, the clubs and our favourite public house and homely conversations', she confided to a friend.

After less than two years in Grafton Terrace, the shine of the new had worn off: 'The situation is now completely unbearable,' Karl wrote to Engels, '... I am completely disabled as far as work goes, partly because I lose most of my time in useless running around trying to make money and partly ... because my power of intellectual concentration is undermined by domestic problems. My wife's nerves are quite ruined by the filth.'

On at least one occasion Karl tried to find paid employment, other than freelance newspaper work, and applied for a job as a clerk with the Great Western Railway, only to be rejected because of his bad handwriting.

Grafton Terrace concealed more than respectable poverty. Karl chaffed also at the constraints imposed by his family, confiding in Engels that 'there is no greater absurdity than for people of general aspirations to marry and surrender themselves to the small miseries of domestic

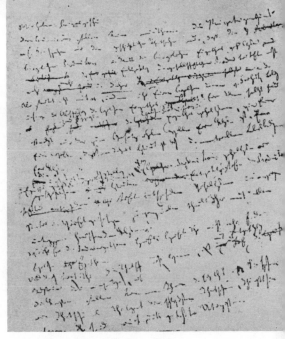

Marx's illegible handwriting

and private life'. One of the miseries was occasioned by smallpox that ravaged Jenny in 1860; so that for a time the children were moved out to stay with the Liebknechts, also living in Kentish Town. Later, at the age of six Eleanor had jaundice, turning the whole family, as she put it, into her 'bond slaves'. Further miseries were in store for Karl himself, when he suffered tortures from crops of boils all over his body. He bore his afflictions with courage, although he naturally told Engels all about them and about his disorders of eyes, liver and 'nerves' – which at least made a change from the constant complaint of poverty.

In 1861 Karl lost a major source of livelihood when the *New York Daily Tribune*, caught in the American Civil War, cut down the number of articles it required from him, and the following year ceased its connection with him. He turned to his Dutch uncle for help, this time successfully. He also borrowed £250 from Ernest Dronke, an old friend from his days in the

Communist League. Yet in January 1863 he was explaining to Engels that he intended to go bankrupt, to turn his elder daughters into governesses, to dismiss Lenchen, and to move into a lodging house with his wife and Eleanor.

Just when most necessary, new sources of income arrived. In the middle of the winter of 1863–4 he received a substantial bequest on his mother's death of almost £600, and in May 1864 his old friend in Manchester, Wilhelm Wolff, whom he had first met in Brussels in 1846, died leaving him the residue of his estate – over £800 (Engels was left £100).

Soon the Marxes were able to move around the corner to an altogether larger, detached house, 1 **Modena Villas** to be renamed 1 **Maitland Park Road** (see map on page 58). The Maitland Park Estate had been developed between 1845 and 1855 – you can still see the remains of the old Orphanage gateway – and the Marxes were comfortable there. The house was bombed in the Second World War, however, and so badly damaged that it had to be pulled down; during the late 1950s the entire site was cleared, and is now occupied by six-storey blocks of flats erected by the former London County Council – a form of municipal socialism that might not have appealed to Marx the revolutionary. (The 1939–45 War did almost as much to alter the landscape of London as the Victorian railways.)

In Maitland Park Road the Marxes had two dogs, three cats and two birds, and for the first time each child had a separate room. Within a few months, the girls, Jenny, Laura, and Eleanor, were to hold a ball for fifty of their friends. The chief delight for Karl was his study, a splendid room overlooking Maitland Park. His future son-in-law, Paul Lafargue, a mulatto born in Cuba, who visited the house for the first

Maitland Park Road just prior to demolition

time in 1865 described it in detail: 'Opposite the window and on either side of the fireplace, the walls were lined with bookcases filled with books and stacked up to the ceiling with newspapers and manuscripts. Opposite the fireplace on one side of the window were two tables piled up with papers, books and newspapers; in the

Paul Lafargue, Marx's son-in-law

Maitland Park Road

proletarian set-up would be unsuitable here,' he went on, 'however fine it might have been when my wife and I were alone or when the children were young'.

When Engels retired from business in 1869 he secured Marx's position by providing him with £100 in capital to pay off his debts and an allowance of £350 a year in quarterly instalments. Thereafter, the Marxes were able to keep up appearances as they wished. Karl was a respected figure in the neighbourhood by the late 1860s. The St Pancras Vestry Minutes record also that in March 1868 the General Purposes Committee had included him in a list of seventy ratepayers whom it wished to enroll as 'Constables for the said Parish for the ensuing year' – 'Ward 1 . . . Charles Marx, 1 Modena Villas . . .' As a foreigner,

middle of the room, well in the light, stood a small, plain desk (three foot by two) and a wooden armchair; between the armchair and the bookcase, opposite the window, was a leather sofa on which Marx used to lie down for a rest from time to time. On the mantelpiece were more books, cigars, matches, tobacco boxes, paperweights and photographs of Marx's daughters and wife, Wilhelm Wolff and Friedrich Engels.'

Not surprisingly, such comfort and space did not come cheaply – the house was twice as expensive to run as 46 Grafton Terrace – and Karl felt 'as hard-up as a church mouse': as early as January 1866, he was grumbling that he had 'minus zero' to sustain his family. In 1868, when financial problems were looming large again, he was summoned for non-payment of rates. He justified his way of life often to Engels, once writing that he was sustained in his difficulties by the thought that 'we two are executing a combined task in which I give my time to the theoretical and party political side of the business. A purely

Marx in 1866

Marx was happy to refuse. When six years later, he applied for British citizenship, the Home Office refused him on the basis not of local evidence but of a police report that he was 'the notorious German agitator who had not been loyal to his own king and country'.

The Marxes hoped that their children would 'enter into connections which can secure them a future'. They had doubts, therefore, when Laura married Lafargue in April 1868 and moved to Paris (Jenny wished Laura had married an Englishman or a German, not a Frenchman, and in the light of her own experience did not wish Laura or Eleanor to become 'political wives'). Five years later, Eleanor, whose future was also causing them anxiety, obtained a teaching post at a boarding school in Brighton. In 1872 Jenny, the eldest daughter, married Jean Longuet, a survivor of the Paris Commune, a French socialist and a London medical student. Marx approved of their union.

Finally in 1875 the Marxes themselves moved for the last time, just along the road to **41 Maitland Park Road** (see map below). This house, too, has disappeared. There has been as much twentieth-century change in the nineteenth-century suburbs of London as in the centre of the city itself, although the railway territory remains the same. The places that have changed least, as Liebknecht noted, are the places of recreation, and these played an important part in the life, not only of the Marx family, but of Karl himself.

GRAFTON TERRACE

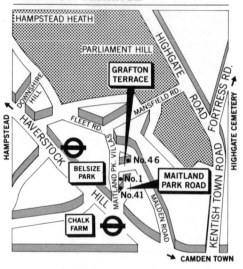

How to get there:

Grafton Terrace (Fitzroy Road), NW1 and *Maitland Park Road (Modena Villas) NW3:* by underground to Chalk Farm station (Northern line)
by bus – routes: **24, 31, 46, 64**

Please note that the Maitland Park Road houses were bombed in the Second World War and no longer exist.

Jenny Marx and her daughter Laura

8
High Days And Holidays

Life for revolutionary exiles in England was not all one long slog of making and unmaking revolutions. Indeed, Liebknecht first met Marx not at a meeting, but at a summer picnic of the German Workers' Education Society. Engels, exiled in smoky Manchester, liked nothing better than to follow the traditional pursuit of the English country gentleman – fox hunting – in his case with the Cheshire Hunt.

Karl's own leisure pursuits were less traditional, but essentially those of a typical German student, and in his early years in London he fenced at a 'salon' in Rathbone Place, off Oxford Street. His taste for wine, like that of Engels, went back to his early student years also. With a public house, the Lord Southampton, at the corner of Grafton Terrace, we can only surmise that many a happy hour was spent inside. Liebknecht mentions specifically other inns in Kentish Town – 'the Old Red Cap so called from a picture of little Red Riding Hood ... and the Mother Shipton'. (He himself lived in Kentish Town at 3 Roxburgh Terrace.)

Liebknecht also described a drinking spree in central London, when he, Karl and another German exile, Edgar Bauer, visited every public house along the Tottenham Court Road. Today the Tottenham Court Road is mainly known as a place to buy furniture and electronic equipment, and there are few pubs, but the rate books show a total of eighteen then. The three revolutionaries were soon thrown out of the last pub, after being drawn into a typical pub argument about the rival claims to fame of England and Germany. This did not lower their spirits, and after a policeman heard them smashing street lamps, they had to rely on Karl's intimate knowledge of the topography of central London to shake off the police and make their way home and not to prison.

Engels and the Marxes – Karl, Jenny, Eleanor and Laura in 1864

A scene inside a mid-Victorian public house

Beer, not wine, seems to have been Karl's main drink at this time, as it was of English working-men. Between 1830 and 1869 beer houses could be opened without a licence from the Justice of the Peace, and very heavy drinking was prevalent. Despite his own tastes, Engels described 'intemperance in the enjoyment of intoxicating liquors' as the principal failing of the English working classes.

In one of the most popular surveys of London, in 1851, Charles Knight claimed that 'beer is to the London citizen what the water in the reservoirs of the plains of Lombardy is to the village peasantry'. Of course, the fact that London water was so unhealthy made the work of the Metropolitan Free Drinking Fountain Association as suspect as that of the brewers, with the great philanthropist, Lord Shaftesbury, noting as late as 1871 that there was scarcely a pint of water in London which was 'not distinctly unhealthy'.

Marx, who took part in a Hyde Park demonstration against the Sunday Observance laws, which Shaftesbury supported, loved the commodity which often went with beer – tobacco. He was a 'passionate smoker' particularly of cigars, and the various homes he inhabited must have been heavy with stale tobacco smoke. Most of the cigars he smoked were very cheap, and he liked to 'save' money by insisting on the lowest price brands. It was perhaps to get away from the smoke of his own house as much as the smoke of central London that the Marxes, when they lived in Soho, would escape each Sunday northwards to the green fields of **Hampstead Heath** (see map on page 65). There he was able to relax.
'A Sunday on Hampstead Heath was the highest pleasure to us,' Liebknecht wrote. 'The children spoke of it all week and grown people too anticipated it with joy. The trip itself was a feast. From Dean Street, where Marx lived, it was at least an

Holiday crowds on Hampstead Heath

hour and a quarter, and as a rule, a start was made as early as 11 a.m. . . . some time was always consumed in getting everything in readiness, the chicken cared for and the basket packed. That basket . . . it was our commissary department, and when a man has a healthy strong stomach . . . then the question of provisions plays a very large role. And good Lenchen knew this and had for often half-starved and, therefore, hungry guests a sympathising heart. A mighty roast veal was the centrepiece hallowed by tradition for the Sunday in Hampstead Heath.'

Liebknecht's description is detailed enough to give an almost complete picture of a London Sunday, far away from the empty central streets and the closed entertainments, and what he wrote of the Dean Street days was equally true of the early days in Kentish Town.

'The march itself was generally accomplished in the following order. I led in the van with the two girls – now telling stories, now executing callisthenics . . . Behind us some friends. Then the main body of the army, Marx and his wife and some Sunday guest requiring special attention. And behind these Lenchen . . . Once arrived on the Heath, we would first choose a place where we could spread our tents at the same time having due regard to the possibility of obtaining tea and beer. But after drinking and eating their fill, as Homer has it, the male and female comrades looked for the most comfortable place of repose or seat; and when this had been found he or she – provided they did not prefer a little nap – produced the Sunday papers they had bought on the road, and now began the reading and discussing of politics – while the children, who rapidly found comrades, played hide and seek behind the heather bushes. But this easy life had to be seasoned by a little diversion, and so we ran races, sometimes we also had wrestling matches, or putting the shot (stones) or some other sport . . .

Jack Straw's castle, then a favourite public house of Marx and friends

The walk home from Hampstead Heath was always very merry, although a pleasure we have enjoyed does not, as a rule, awaken as agreeable feelings as one we are expecting. Against melancholy – although there were only too many good reasons for it – we were charmed by our irrepressible humour. The misery of exile did not exist for us – whoever began to complain was at once reminded in the most impressive manner of his social duties.'

If these were rural pleasures, the Marxes enjoyed urban pleasures too, particularly the theatre. They would often walk from Haverstock Hill to Sadler's Wells in Holborn to see Shakespeare, and they were deeply impressed by Henry Irving, whom they saw (and heard) as Hamlet at the Lyceum in 1874. (Marx sent a Lyceum ticket in 1877 – for a performance of *Richard III* – to a Russian exile, Peter Lavrov). Eleanor joined the New Shakespeare Society, recited to the Browning Society (once picnicking down the Thames with the members), and took to the stage. She had always been a lively and entertaining person, and it was characteristic of her that when she was ten, and in a popular game of the period produced her 'Confession', she replied to the question 'what is your idea of happiness?' – 'champagne.'

Karl was interested in all her doings. He was, indeed, a good and caring father. One of his favourite games was playing 'Cavalry' with a child on his shoulders. Throughout his life, he saw to it as far as he possibly could that however much he and Jenny might have to suffer through their poverty, their children would not have to suffer too. Indeed, in their aspirations for the children – private schooling at the South Hampstead Ladies College, piano lessons, dancing and lots of reading – Karl and Jenny were not revolutionary but bourgeois.

Engels never had this family sense. His free union with the Irish factory girl, Mary Burns, and later (on her death) with her sister, Lizzie, left no place for children, although Lizzie welcomed the Marx children and showed them round

Manchester. Eleanor remembered one summer day when all the female members of the household were lying on the floor 'the whole day drinking beer, claret, etc . . . with no stays, no boots, no petticoat and a cotton dress on' and by the time Engels returned they were 'drunk as a jelly'.

Engels used to visit Karl regularly in London, too, before he came to live there himself, and once he had to write to Jenny apologising for leading Karl astray: he received the answer that since their 'nocturnal wanderings' Karl had been confined to bed for a week with an alleged chill.

Real illness certainly affected the leisure pattern of the Marxes, as it affected the leisure pattern of most Victorians. In 1874 he visited the spa at Karlsbad (now called Karlovy Vary) staying (as Herr Charles Marx, Privatier) at the Germanic Hotel. 'We are very exact indeed in all our "duties" (i.e. taking the waters)', wrote Eleanor, who accompanied him, 'being fully dressed and out at the "Brunnen" (springs) by six o'clock, frequently still

Marx in middle age, 1872

Eleanor in early adulthood

earlier. We take long walks, and altogether get on well here.'

It was for reasons of health, too, which took Karl to Algiers and Monte Carlo in 1881, to Geneva in 1882 and, nearer to home, to Ventnor in the Isle of Wight. Ventnor, renowned for its air, was no more a proletarian holiday resort than Monte Carlo, although it had been graced by Herzen for a whole summer in 1854. Marx's German contemporary, Karl Baedecker, described it in his *London and its Environs, including Excursions to Brighton, the Isle of Wight* etc (1879) as having a winter climate 'almost Italian in its mildness'. It was, he added, 'much frequented by persons suffering from complaints of the chest'.

Another non-proletarian resort favoured by Karl was Eastbourne, developed under the patronage of the Duke of Devonshire. It was the most respectable seaside resort on the south coast, more respectable than Brighton to the west and Hastings to the east, which he also visited, or Margate, which could be approached by river down

the Thames. The river world of London was a pleasure world as well as a working world – with Richmond to the west and Southend to the east.

Another very respectable place visited by the Marxes was Harrogate, not far from Bradford and Leeds, but very different from them – a spa, not a popular resort, and recommended by a doctor friend.

Engels once went on holiday not to Blackpool, in Lancashire, but to Great Yarmouth. Neither Marx nor Engels followed, therefore, the work and leisure patterns of 'the masses', already plain in the year of revolutions, 1848, when in the short Whitsuntide break, a yearly festival in the life of the working classes, 116,000 trippers left Manchester for the sea. By the time of Karl's death, a visit to the seaside

The house in Ventnor, Isle of Wight, where Marx spent his last period of convalescence

Margate as the Marxes would have found it 1873

(for very different reasons from taking the waters) had become a fact of urban life.

'The masses', 'a human ocean', figure in Liebknecht's *Memoirs*, in a non-political way, when he describes a visit with two Marx daughters, to the Duke of Wellington's funeral procession in 1852. 'Take good care of the children! Don't mix up with the crowd,' Jenny warned him as he went out. Once among the crowd, Liebknecht felt himself compelled 'to resist with all my strength, trying to protect the children so that the torrent will rush by without touching them.' There was a hint of a political moral in the story, however, 'In vain. Against the elemental forces of the masses, no human strength will avail.'

HAMPSTEAD HEATH

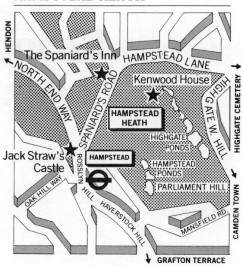

How to get there:

Hampstead Heath, NW3: by underground to Hampstead station (Northern line); by British Rail to Hampstead Heath Station (on the Broad Street to Richmond line)
by bus – routes: **24, 46, 187, 210, 214, 268, CII.**

9
Revolution
In Covent Garden

Covent Garden (see map on page 74) was the centre of the main political events of Marx's life during the 1860s. It is very near to London's theatreland and houses the great Opera House which was rebuilt after a fire in the years 1856–1888. There is no evidence that Marx ever went there, nor is there any evidence that he wandered round the famous Covent Garden fruit and vegetable market, which was moved to Battersea in 1974. There had been demands for the removal of the market as early as the 1860s, and the area has now at last been converted into a place for visitors. There are still a few houses left for the workers in the area, but most of the premises are occupied by fashionable boutiques, wine bars, restaurants, and advertising agencies – though there are still open-air stalls.

The visitors in the 1850s and early 1860s included a group of socialists, so that Covent Garden, an even more unlikely place from which to plot revolution than Soho, figures prominently for a time in Marx's biography. The reason why was the existence of **St Martin's Hall** (see map on page 74) in Long Acre, not far from the market, where the first 'International' met on 25 September 1864.

St Martin's Hall, long since pulled down, had itself been rebuilt and reopened in 1862 after a fire. First opened in 1850 from the proceeds of a testimonial fund in honour of John Hullah, pioneer of 'music for the masses' – and the scene of many concerts – it was now, not for the first time, to be used for a political appeal to the masses.

Marx had been invited to at least one of the earliest political events in February 1855, when 'the 1848 alliance of all

The First International, London 1864

Covent Garden today, the central market

peoples' was commemorated, but he had refused to go because of the presence of Herzen, adding, 'I am not of the opinion that "old Europe" can be rejuvenated by Russian blood'. Two years later, there was a two-week conference at the Hall, called by the eighty-year-old British Utopian socialist, Robert Owen.

The year 1864 was a significant year in the history of nineteenth-century English protest. In particular, London politics, which had been relatively quiet for fifteen years, following the decline of Chartism, quickened again. The change in mood was partly provoked by the American Civil War, when many English workers supported the American North ('new and brilliant proof of the indestructible excellence of the English popular masses', wrote Marx (in an unusual tribute) and partly inspired by the Polish insurrection against the Russians in 1863. 1864 above

all, was the year of the visit to London of the great Italian liberator, Garibaldi, who received a more enthusiastic reception from the London crowds than any visiting foreign politician had ever done. Garibaldi, who spoke in St Martin's Hall, was received by a procession of as many as fifty thousand people who were organised by trade unionists in the London Trades Council, set up in 1860.

It is impossible to understand the ferment of the year, therefore, without taking account of the strikingly recent growth in British trade unionism. The leadership of the Amalgamated Society of Engineers, founded in 1851, worked very closely with the leadership of the Amalgamated Society of Carpenters and Joiners, founded in 1860, and both of them with the Builders, who were engaged in bitter struggles with their employers between 1850 and 1861. These were the

Garibaldi's Reception at the Crystal Palace, April 1864

key groups in the formation in 1860 of the London Trades Council, which secured its first great success in 1861 when it persuaded the government to withdraw soldiers sent into Chelsea Barracks to replace builders on strike there.

Practical trade-union concerns in the early 1860s – including the demand for a nine-hour working day – suggested the need for working-class solidarity, including solidarity with workers in all parts of Britain and with workers overseas, particularly in neighbouring France, if only to check the use of cheap non-unionised foreign labour by employers. But the practical concerns were reinforced by political enthusiasms also, for many of the protesters were interested not only in industrial legislation but, as the Chartists had been, in the right to vote.

'Never,' indeed, wrote an old Chartist in 1864, 'have the relations between capital

and labourers been in so disturbed and agitated a state as at the present time.' These lines appeared in the weekly *Beehive* newspaper, founded in 1861 by George Potter 'in the interest of the working classes'.

The forces of discontent converged in a great London meeting on 25 September 1864, attended by a deputation of French trade-unionists, in St Martin's Hall, Long Acre, when addresses from the working classes of one country to the other were exchanged, and it was proposed that an international association should be formed to promote peace and foster the common interests of the working classes of all countries. There had been an earlier meeting in July 1863 at St James's Hall, which was attended by a five-man delegation from the Paris Working Man's Polish Committee, followed by discussions in the Bell Inn, the editorial headquarters of the *Beehive*. The 1864 meeting came, therefore, as a dramatic climax.

Marx had not been involved in the

An early trades union banner

planning of this historic event; indeed, he had tended to avoid any direct political activity in Britain itself during his long years of exile. He had concentrated on his studies and on confrontation at a distance with other European socialist theoreticians – notably P. J. Proudhon in France and his old friend, the German socialist Ferdinand Lasalle – with whom he finally broke in 1860. Now, however, Marx appreciated that the workers of the country were beginning to talk to each other as he had always demanded.

Marx sat 'mute' during the first meeting, receiving his invitation from a British trade unionist – as a representative of the German workers – only a few hours before the meeting took place. Yet it was he who drafted the Inaugural Address of what was now called the International Working Men's Association, which he described as 'a sort of review of the adventures of the working classes since 1845'.

The address was, indeed, the most important socialist document since the

A contemporary satire on Proudhon and his theories on property

Communist Manifesto, from which it differed substantially, with most of its propositions supported by specific British evidence, but it ended, as in 1848, with the words 'Proletarians of all countries unite'. It stated firmly also that 'the subjection of the man of labour to the man of capital lies at the bottom of all servitude, all social misery, and all political dependence'.

St Martin's Hall ultimately made way for one of the many publishers' offices that used to dot Covent Garden, among them by coincidence, that of Odhams Press which published the twentieth-century labour newspaper the *Daily Herald*, founded in 1911. Now most of these publishers' offices too have been demolished, and the *Daily Herald* has been defunct since 1964.

The International Working Men's Association, as constituted in September 1864, had a very eclectic membership – ranging from revolutionaries like Marx and Eccarius, who had worked with Marx in the Communist League to the Positivists, followers of the French sociologist Auguste Comte. They believed that it was important to create new forms of solidarity between workers and thinkers. One of their English leaders, Professor Beesley, took the chair at many working-class meetings; and was on good terms with working trade-unionists like W. R. Cremer, the first IWMA secretary, a member of the Amalgamated Society of Carpenters and Joiners.

There were twenty-seven Englishmen on its first General Council, of whom at least eleven were from the building trades.

Marx did not become a member until 5 October 1864, but five days later when there were three French members of the Council, two Italians and two Germans, the final draft of the rules was written by Marx and completed in a late-night session at his Maitland Park house. Its provisional

The two sides of the International.

Below: agenda with Poland and Russia actively debated

Right: the lighter side, the soirée programme

AL COUNCIL, when the fol
ill be discussed :—

6.-- Direct and indirect taxation.
7.— Reduction of the number of the hours of labour.
8.— Female and children's labour.
9.—The Muscovite invasion of Europe, and the re-establishment of an integral and independent Poland.
10.—Standing Armies: their effects upon the interests of the productive classes from the various Working Men's Associations in Europe and America.

o'Clock at 18. Greek Street: Trade. Friendly

rules had made no direct reference to socialism, but the emancipation of the working man was identified as 'the great end to which every political movement ought to be subordinated as a means'.

The International was organised on different levels. For the ordinary trade union member his card might be his only real link. But a union, as a whole, could be centrally affiliated to the governing bodies of the International.

The subjects discussed in the various sessions of the International in 1864 were wide-ranging and many of them are of more than historical interest. They included industrial arbitration; the past, present and future of trade unions; the fight for a shorter working day; Ireland; and European foreign policy, with one topic being defined as 'the Muscovite invasion of Europe and the re-establishment of an integral and independent Poland'.

It would have been impossible for the International to have discussed this range of topics in most European capital cities in

1864. Even in Switzerland, it has been pointed out, strikes were treated as abnormalities and in Belgium as acts of war. There was no national trade-union organisation in Napoleon III's France, though strikes were made legal in 1864, and in Germany there was virtually no collective bargaining outside the printing trade. Moreover, as Applegarth, the leader of the British carpenters, proudly told the delegates, 'fortunately we have no need of creeping into holes and corners lest a policeman should see us'.

The men of the International did not only engage in earnest discussion, at their first sessions in 1864. There were other distractions, too, such as a soirée on 28 September. The programme included tea at half-past seven with music from the band of the Italian Working Men's Association, followed by addresses from foreign delegates, songs from a German chorus and 'at half past ten dancing – 3 polkas, 3 quadrilles and 12 other dances.' And, to help the evening

A SOIREE

Will be held in

ST. MARTIN'S HALL,

LONG ACRE,

To Celebrate the FOUNDATION of the ASSOCIATION to Welcome the CONTINENTAL DELEGATES and to propose an Address of CON-
GRATULATION to the PEOPLE of AMERICA on their ABOLITION of SLAVERY and the TRIUMPH OF THE REPUBLIC

**The Entertainment will consist of Tea, Choruses by the German Work-
ing Men's Choral Society, Operatic and other selections by the Band
of the Italian Working Men's Association, Dancing, etc.**

**During the Evening short addresses will be delivered by the continental
Delegates.**

**Tickets· to admit at half-past 7, including Tea, Concert,
Addresses and Dancing, One Shilling.**

**Tickets to admit after Tea at half-past 8, to Concert, Ad-
dresses and Dancing, Six-pence.**

DANCING AT HALF-PAST TEN.

International Working Men's Association.

CENTRAL COUNCIL,

18 GREEK STREET, LONDON, W.

—o♦o—

Trade, Friendly, or any Working Men's Societies are invited to join in their corporate capacity, the only conditions being that the Members subscribe to the principles of the Association, and pay for the declaration of their enrolment (which is varnished and mounted on canvas and roller), the sum of 5s. No contributions are *de-manded* from Societies joining, it being left to their means and discretion to contribute or not, or as they may from time to time deem the *efforts* of the *Association worthy of support.*

The Central Council will be pleased to send the Address and Rules, which fully explain the principles and aims of the Association, to any Society applying for them : and, if within the London district, deputations will gladly attend to afford any further information that may be required. Societies joining are entitled to send a representative to the Central Council. The amount of contribution for individual members is 1s. per annum, with 1d. for Card of Membership; which may be obtained; with every information concerning the Association, by applying to the Honorary Secretary, or at the Central Council's Meetings, which are held every Tuesday Evening, at 18 Greek Street, from Eight to Ten o'clock.

E. DUPONT, *Corresponding Secretary for* France.
K. MARX, „ „ Germany.
E. HOLTORP, „ „ Poland.
H. IUNG, „ „ Switzerland.
L. LEWIS, „ „ America

G. ODGER, *President of Central Council*
G. W. WHEELER, *Hon. Treasurer.*
W. R. CREMER, *Hon. Gen. Sec.*

along, 'wines, spirits, ales, stout, tea, coffee, etc', were to be sold 'at tavern prices'.

Between the subsequent annual assemblies of the International held in different places in Europe, it was left to the General Council in London to carry on the work. It met from eight to ten o'clock, at first every Thursday evening, then every Tuesday evening, in time for its news to reach the weekly papers. Its first meeting place was the front room of 18 Greek Street, Soho (just around the corner from Marx's old Dean Street home), rented at £12 per year. Its members were soon faced, however, with the same sort of financial problems with which Marx was so familiar, and in October 1865 they repaired to the back room which was £2 cheaper. But not for long. In April 1866 there was a further move to a room in the offices of the Industrial Newspaper Company in Bouverie Street, off Fleet Street, where the new newspaper of the International called *Commonwealth*, was published.

The results of the 1871 Paris Commune

write *Wages, Prices and Profit* as a counterweight to the growing influence of Proudhon amongst the French socialists, and in the same year, the followers of the Italian, Mazzini, were driven out of the International. 1865 was also the year in which the International was at its peak in England – a year, too, when the Reform

IWMA card signed by Marx

Although throwing himself deeply into the work of the International, Marx never accepted high office. When Cremer was unable to attend meetings, however, Marx's friend and loyal supporter Eccarius would take the chair, and Marx himself was, from the start, the corresponding secretary for Germany, the country of his birth and the one which still interested him most. This meant that he had a new link with Liebknecht – the International's 'man on the ground' in Germany – through whom he could report the progress of the movement in his homeland to the Central Council. Later, he was also given the task of being the corresponding secretary for Russia too, not a country he knew from first-hand experience.

Marx saw his main task as getting the International to think and act along 'Marxist' lines. To this end, he conducted energetic and often vituperative campaigns against rival ideologists. In 1865, he was to

League was founded in London to press for manhood suffrage. Six members of the General Council of the International served on the League's Permanent Committee.

The membership of the International was never very large, and the minute books, very carefully kept in a characteristically British way, report the Association's annual income in September 1865 at 'Only £33' (about one fifth of Marx's annual allowance from Engels).

There was a decline in British support after the passing of the Reform Act of 1867, which extended the suffrage to many working men, and there were few further British trade-union affiliations. Ironically at this time, however, the International acquired new strength on the Continent. Two events in the early 1870s were to lead to its eventual demise. The Franco-Prussian War of 1870 like the First World War forty years later – showed the strength

The destruction of the column in the Place Vendôme during the 1871 Paris Commune

of national rather than class feeling. More significantly, the Paris Commune of 1871, formed by working-men after the collapse of the French armies and the abdication and flight of Napoleon III plunged the International into controversy. Seen by hostile observers and governments at the time as the master stroke of the 'secret' International Association, it proved in fact to be its zenith and nadir simultaneously.

Marx's brilliant work of instant journalism on these events *The Civil War in France*, sold very well throughout Europe and brought Marx into the middle of the revolutionary limelight. He soon found himself, indeed, in his own words, 'the best calumniated and menaced man in London' (adding in a letter 'That really does one good after a tedious twenty years idyll in my den'.)

Most English trade-union leaders did not share Marx's view that the Commune was 'a new point of departure of world-

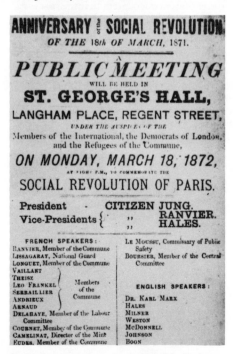

An anniversary commemoration of the Paris Commune featuring Marx as speaker

historic importance'. They disliked what they thought of as its excesses and separated themselves from the work of the International, so that by September 1871, when the International met for a last time in London, at an inn just off the Tottenham Court Road, there were present only refugees from France and two Englishmen.

At this time, the targets for Marx's vitriol were the Russian anarchist Michael Bakunin and his followers, whose visions both of revolution and socialism were very different from his own.

Despite Marx's optimism, the International was to struggle on for only one more year in Europe. At its Hague conference in 1872, Engels, who had not joined the Council until 1870 (then in the unlikely role as corresponding secretary for Spain, Portugal and Italy), proposed, and the conference accepted, that the seat of the General Council be transferred to New York. In order to save the International from rival ideologists Marx had effectively destroyed it, and four years later it was formally dissolved in Philadelphia.

COVENT GARDEN

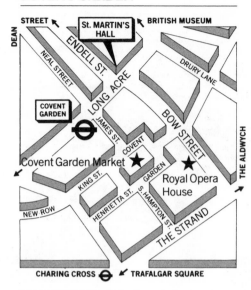

How to get there:

Long Acre, WC2 and *Covent Garden Market, WC2:* by underground to Covent Garden Station (Piccadilly line, closed Sundays); Leicester Square Station (Northern and Piccadilly lines); Charing Cross Station (Jubilee, Bakerloo and Northern lines); Holborn Station (Piccadilly and Central lines).
by bus – routes: 1, 6, 9, 11, 13, 15, 23, 24, 29, 77, 77a, 170, 176

Please note that St Martin's Hall no longer stands.

10
Death
In Highgate

During the last ten years of his life, after the collapse of the International, Marx was settling into the routines of an old man, as many of the people he had known best disappeared from the scene. As early as 1864, on the death of the German socialist Ferdinand Lassalle, whose views were different from his own, he complained to Engels how 'the crowd is getting even smaller and no new blood is being added.' Sometimes he would attend a London funeral, like that of John Rogers, a tailor and the President of the Manhood Suffrage League, at Finchley cemetery in 1877.

His meal times were regular and he took frequent walks on Hampstead Heath, often with his old friend Engels, who from 1870 to 1895 lived nearby at **122 Regent's Park Road** (see endpapers), close to Primrose Hill (Jenny had helped him find the house). In the last year of his life, long after Marx was dead, Engels was to move very near to the Zoological Gardens in Regent's Park.

Like so many people of sedentary, nocturnal habits, and given to smoking and drink, Karl had misused his physique. Into his sixties he had impressed people he met as a powerful, untamed man, whose sparkling brown eyes displayed tremendous intelligence, but the last ten years of his life were years of increasingly debilitating ill health. One of the doctors

he consulted attributed the complaints to poor nourishment and over-work and prescribed regular meals, compulsory exercise and wine with soda. He also managed for a time to limit Marx's working day, when he was fit to work at all, to only two hours in the morning and two hours in the evening.

Yet Marx was restless under such conditions, and in 1875, for example, rallied himself to write a strong criticism of the Gotha Programme drafted by the German Social Democrats. He even began

Friedrich Engels in his later years

Marx with his favourite daughter, Jenny

Above: Jenny Marx just before her death in 1881
Right: the last-known photograph of Karl Marx,
Algiers 1882

to learn Russian. (A translation into
Russian of *Das Kapital* appeared in 1872.)

The visits he made on medical advice to
watering places and to spas (Harrogate and
Malvern as well as Karlsbad) brought only
temporary relief, for his health always
broke down again once he had returned to
London. Moreover, to this list of troubles,
he had to add growing concern over his
wife's worsening health. Cancer of the
liver, 'a beastly illness', finally confined her
to bed. 'That was a terrible time,' Eleanor
wrote later. 'Our dear mother lay in the big
front room, Moor in the small room next to
it. They who were so much to each other,
whose lives had come to form part of each
other, could not even be in the same room
together.'

Eventually Jenny died in Karl's
presence in December 1881, her last word

being 'good'. She was sixty-seven years of
age. It was a terrible blow to him, for, since
he was a teenager, Jenny had shared all his
hopes, disappointments and hardships as
well as many happy times together. Despite
all their troubles and up and downs, they
were close to each other to the moment of
her death. Karl could not attend her
funeral because he had very recently been
in bed with pleurisy and bronchitis and the
weather was appalling, and it was Engels,
who had shown 'kindness and devotion
that beggared description', who delivered
a short speech over her grave. In it he
claimed eloquently that she had 'lived to
see the calumny which had showered down
upon her husband scattered like chaff
before the wind'. Yet he offended Eleanor
by saying – and she believed it – that Karl
was now dead too. It was true. Karl

The Marxes' original grave in Highgate Cemetery

received many warm letters of condolence paying tribute to Jenny's character and urging him to soldier on despite his dreadful loss. Yet he lived for only another fifteen months.

The final blow, from which he was never to recover, came with the death, from cancer of the bladder, of Jenny his first born child, after many years of poor health, in January 1883. Again, Engels was on hand to write her obituary, and Eleanor who travelled to Ventnor, where her father was staying, to tell him the news, felt that she was carrying with her her father's final death sentence.

Karl lingered on for two more months, but he now developed laryngitis and a lung tumour to add to his other complaints, and

finally slipped away quietly on 14 March 1883. Engels called at the house in Maitland Park Road soon after two p.m. on that day and was taken by Lenchen up to the study where she had left Karl sleeping. They entered and found him dead in his favourite armchair.

Engels took care of all the funeral arrangements, sending telegrams and letters to announce the death. Marx was buried in the same grave as his wife in **Highgate Cemetery** (see map on page 81), on 17 March 1883. About twenty people were present, among them his son-in-law, Longuet who read a message in French from Peter Lavrov, in the name of the Russian Socialists. It was fitting that the funeral, small though it was, had become

A view of Highgate Cemetery, showing the present position of the Marx tomb. The bodies were moved in 1954 and the memorial bronze erected in 1956

something of an international affair.

'The greatest brain in the second half of our century had ceased to think', Engels wrote to Liebknecht, who represented the German Social Democrats at the funeral and spoke, in German, of Marx as his 'dead, living friend'. It was fitting too – and inevitable – that Engels should deliver the main address. Marx, he said, was one of the group of outstanding men, few of whom are produced in any century. 'Just as Darwin discovered the law of development of organic nature, so Marx discovered the law of development of human history.' The rhetoric continued: 'He died beloved, revered and mourned by millions of revolutionary fellow-workers, from the mines of Siberia to California . . . His name will live on through the centuries and so also will his work.'

The grave where Karl and Jenny were laid to rest was topped only by a simple gravestone showing only their birth and death dates. Yet the cemetery itself, Highgate, was a place of grandeur, a typical expression of Victorian culture. It had been opened to the public two years after Queen Victoria came to the throne in response to the overcrowded, insanitary conditions in the existing city churchyards, as a money-making concern initiated by the London Cemetery Company. Beautiful and profitable, it was more spacious than many residential areas, and it was romantically landscaped too. Its gloomy gardens with broad avenues and grandiose

The Soviet leaders Krushchev and Bulganin pay homage to Marx in 1956

tombs and memorials, sculptured in many different styles and with many different symbols, demonstrate the peculiar attachment of Victorians (including Queen Victoria herself) to their way of death.

Marx was in good company at Highgate, where many eminent Victorians found their final resting place. The novelist George Eliot was buried not far away and there is a memorial also to Dickens. The tomb of Herbert Spencer, the philosopher who wrote *inter alia* that 'socialism is slavery', is one of the closest of all to Marx's in the eastern half of the cemetery.

The Marx grave was moved to a better position in the cemetery in 1954, when it was decided, though Marx had asked for a simple grave, that a more impressive headstone should mark the spot. Laurence

Bradshaw was commissioned by the Communist Party of Great Britain, to sculpt a bronze head of Marx, and the monument which incorporated it was unveiled in 1956 by Harry Pollitt, then Secretary General of the British Communist Party.

Marx's head rests on a huge Cornish granite plinth, which bears the famous exhortion from the *Communist Manifesto*, written by Marx and Engels in 1848, 'Workers of all lands, unite'. At the base of the monument is carved a quotation from his eleventh thesis on the philosopher, Ludwig Feuerbach, written in 1845, 'The philosophers have only *interpreted* the world in various ways. The point however is to change it.'

There have subsequently been many

attempts to change the face of Marx's memorial. Slogans have been regularly daubed over it and cleaned off again, while more violent critics have tried to disfigure it, even to blow it up. It still stands, however, defiant and impervious, begging as many questions as it answers, a sight for visitors, friendly or hostile, from all over the world.

HIGHGATE CEMETERY

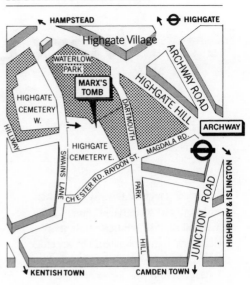

A tablet marks the position of the original grave

How to get there:

Marx's tomb in Highgate Cemetery, Swain's Lane, N6: by underground to Archway Station (Northern line)
by bus – routes: **143, 210, 239, 271, C11**
Opening times: 1 April–30 September.
Mon–Sat 9–5, Sundays and Public Holidays 2–5
1 October–31 March.
Mon–Sat 9–4, Sundays and Public Holidays 1–4

11
Marx Lives On

Marx was survived by only two of his children. His second daughter, Laura married a fellow medical student of Charles Longuet, husband of her elder sister, a Cuban-born Frenchman, Paul Lafargue. Longuet never became a physician but Lafargue qualified in London, although he did not practise in England. Marx had displayed an initial coolness towards Paul Lafargue, though he later came to have a warm regard for his son-in-law. Lenin met him and Laura, too, in Paris in 1895. The three children of the Lafargue marriage all died in infancy, and Laura died with her husband in a tragic 'suicide pact' in 1911.

Marx's youngest surviving child, his favourite, Eleanor, died before her in 1898, so that Laura was the only child left to see the publication of the *Theories of Surplus Value* – sometime known as Volume IV of *Das Kapital* in 1905–10.

Eleanor's interest in the theatre and her career as an actress led to her liaison with Dr Edward Aveling, the socialist and scientist. She lived with him until her death in 1898, but it was an unhappy relationship. She was stunned to learn that Aveling had secretly married another woman, also an actress, under an assumed identity, and she resolved to take her own life. In this macabre episode she was assisted by

Aveling, whose part in the tragedy aroused as much indignation in socialist circles as most of his previous actions had done; he lived but a few months after her.

Eleanor left no children. During her life, she had been prominent in Marxist circles in London as a member first of the Social Democratic Federation, later of William Morris's Socialist League. In 1886 and early 1887 she and Aveling had spent fifteen weeks lecturing in the United States, and on her return she had been drawn into the life of East End radical clubs in London, including the Labour Partriotic Club, which had its headquarters at **37c Clerkenwell Green** (see map on page 93). She took part from there in the demonstrations on 'Bloody Sunday', 13 November 1887 and spoke at a meeting on Clerkenwell Green on 20 October 1889 in support of the London dock strike. She spoke at other meetings on the Green, and was active, too, in the Bloomsbury Socialist Society. In 1896 she rejoined the Social Democratic Federation and contributed regular reports thereafter to its journal *Justice*, which after her suicide published a full-page drawing of her by Walter Crane.

Both Laura and Eleanor were beneficiaries of Engels's will. Together they received three-eighths of the residue of his estate, the considerable sum of £24,000,

Above: Edward Aveling and Marx's youngest daughter, Eleanor

Left: Laura Marx who married Charles Lafargue. Both daughters later committed suicide

Helene Demuth towards the end of her life

tribulations of the Marx family for so many years, died in 1890 and was buried in the same grave as Karl and Jenny.

The saddest tale of all relates to Lenchen's son, Henry Frederick Demuth, born in Dean Street in 1851. He received a working-class upbringing and became a skilled engineering toolmaker in East London. After the death of Marx, when Helene Demuth became housekeeper to Engels, Freddy was allowed to visit his mother, and all three Marx sisters showed an interest in his welfare, although only Eleanor formed a close friendship with him. The girls assumed him to be the illegitimate son of Engels, and the truth did not become known until Engels, on his deathbed, confided to Eleanor that Marx was the father – and then only, as he said, lest he should be spoken ill of afterwards for neglecting his 'son'. At first Eleanor would not believe it. She was shocked, not because her beloved father had been unfaithful to his wife, but because he had been cruel to Freddy, whom she now

but in a letter to them Engels asked them to hold one third of their legacy in trust for the children of their sister, Jenny Longuet, who had died only ten weeks before Marx.

There were six children, of whom four (three boys and one girl – Jean, Edgar, Marcel, and Jenny) survived to a good age. Jean was active in the leadership of the French Socialist Party, an opponent of the First World War and a supporter in 1921 of the so-called 'Two-and-a-half International' founded in Vienna. He, Edgar and Marcel kept the Marx family inheritance alive and fathered Marx's seven great-grandchildren (six boys and one girl). Three of them are still alive, including Robert Jean Longuet, a journalist and biographer of his great-grandfather, who now lives in a Paris apartment once occupied by Balzac. Robert Jean Longuet is not a Marxist. Another Longuet lives in Normandy, a third in Paris.

Helene Demuth, 'Lenchen', the faithful family maid who had borne the trials and

Frederick Demuth as an old man

regarded as her closest friend.

Freddy's own life was not particularly happy, for though he married, his wife deserted him shortly before the First World War.

He had a son, Harry, who soon had three children of his own to keep on twenty-two shillings a week, but on the death of his father at the age of seventy-seven in 1929, he was bequeathed a legacy of nearly £2,000.

12
London After Marx

Marx had died during the early years of one of the most exciting decades of nineteenth-century English history. As the old issues of franchise politics were giving way increasingly to social politics, policy towards Ireland split the Liberal Party of Gladstone in 1886. The new alignments did not calm a country which was passing through difficult economic circumstances – high unemployment, increased foreign competition, distress in the countryside. It was then that the mid-Victorian equilibrium, always precarious, always qualified, was finally broken down.

There was talk again, therefore, for the first time since the 1840s of possible revolution, a 'fiery furnace' through which England would have to pass – and this time much of the talk – and the action – focused not on the provinces, as in the 1840s, but on London, the capital. There were many radical clubs there, some of which had been founded while Marx was still alive, like the Notting Hill Progressive Club (1872) and the Manhood Suffrage League, which had been founded in 1875. During the 1880s there were particularly strong centres of working-class activity in Battersea, south of the river, West Ham to the north-east and in dockland, where the decade ended with one of the most publicised strikes of the nineteenth

century, 'the fight for the dockers' tanner' (sixpence) in 1889.

New personalities were involved in trade union and socialist struggles during the 1880s as the life of Eleanor Marx revealed and as Engels had to recognise. In particular, three new political bodies turned to the propagation of socialism – the Democratic Federation, founded in 1881 by H. M. Hyndman, which changed its name to the Social Democratic Federation in 1883; the Socialist League, a splinter organisation created in 1885 with William Morris as one of its leaders; and the Fabian Society, which emerged from a drawing room discussion group in 1884 and which attracted personalities as different as George Bernard Shaw and Sidney Webb.

In the trade union movement, although London was not a major stronghold, one new union of 1889 appealing to unskilled workers – the National Union of Gas Workers and General Labourers – enrolled eight hundred men within a day and two thousand within a week. The union had its origin in labour disturbances at the Beckton gas works in East Ham, the biggest in the world. The failure of the SDF to see the significance of this trade union growth left it curiously isolated from the currents of change.

A commemoration of the 1889 London Dock Strike

A procession of dockers during the 1889 strike

Engels, who survived Marx by twelve years, watched these and other developments with great interest, although he was preoccupied with finishing *Das Kapital* from Marx's notes and with guiding, from a distance, German social democracy, which in 1891 had a much discussed new programme, the Erfurt programme. He believed that England should have a political party as strong as the German Social Democrats were proving to be, arguing forcefully as early as 1881 – before Marx died – that 'for the full representation of labour in Parliament, as well as for the preparation of the abolition of the wages system, organisations will become necessary, not of separate trades, but of the working class as a body. And the sooner this is done the better. There is no body in the world which could for a day resist the British working class organised as one'.

Engels had great reservations about the Social Democratic Federation, however, as led by Hyndman, 'the socialist in the top hat', even though Hyndman took up many of Marx's doctrines, and he was equally concerned later about anarchist elements in the Socialist League, which itself was to split. Morris's socialism had much in common with that of Marx – even in its independent strands, which revealed parallel thinking and feeling – but his personality as a leader did not impress Engels. Above all, Engels was anxious to restrain too confident hopes of imminent revolution in revolutionary exile circles in London as well as among London working men. He was prepared to press flexibly for short-term objectives which would attract voters.

Thus, socialism, while increasing its appeal during the 1880s, was characterised

H. M. Hyndman, an early British Socialist

William Morris

by fierce in-fighting. Rank-and-file members might belong to organisations whose leaders were arguing bitterly with each other. Yet the disputes between the leaders could never be discounted: Hyndman refused to speak, for example, at a meeting arranged at Marx's grave in 1884.

One of the most active and controversial participants in the arguments was Dr Edward Aveling, whose love affair with Eleanor Marx complicated the politics. It was at Aveling's house, that the decision to split off the Socialist League from the SDF was taken, and when the anarchists seemed to be taking charge of the League in 1888, Aveling and Eleanor decided to convert the Bloomsbury branch of the League into the Bloomsbury Socialist Society. Aveling, whose dubious character was known to all his comrades, was portrayed in George

Edward and Eleanor Aveling

George Bernard Shaw (right) with Keir Hardie during the 1910 General Election campaign

Bernard Shaw's play *The Doctor's Dilemma* (1906) as Dubedat.

In 1893 yet another new labour party was to be founded – the Independent Labour Party – not in London but in Bradford – by the Scot Keir Hardie. In 1892 he had been elected MP for West Ham, the first London Independent Labour MP, and, although, he was defeated in 1895, the new ILP was to prove far more successful as a party than the SDF. It offered a gospel rather than a theory, and it was to take the lead, along with trade unionists and other sections of the Labour movement, in summoning on 27 February 1900, a historically significant meeting at the Memorial Hall, Farringdon Street, where the Labour Representative Committee, later to be known as the Labour Party, was formed.

The years between 1883 and 1900 can be examined in detail – largely from the pages of new Labour journals like *Justice*, founded by Hyndman in 1884, and *Commonwealth*, the organ of the Socialist League, launched by Morris in 1885. (The Fabians produced their subsequently famous volume of *Essays* in 1889.) There was also an increasingly probing non-socialist literature about London, which acquired a new County Council in 1888. Hyndman himself assembled a mass of facts about the city and its problems, but so, too, did the non-socialist Charles Booth, whose massive survey, in sixteen volumes *The Life and Labour of the People of London*, the first volume of which appeared in 1892, reveals both the immense variety of human circumstances in London and the distinctive features of each of its constituent parts.

Within London, which Booth described as 'unrivalled national emporium and mother city of the Kingdom and of the Empire', there was still a place for revolutionary exiles from Europe. Prince Kropotkin, the anarchist, who arrived for the first time in 1876 and settled in London permanently in 1886, was one. He was to stay in London almost as long as Marx had – until 1917. In 1883, the year of Marx's death, another Russian terrorist,

Prince Peter Kropotkin

wife, 'he loved going long rides about the town on top of an omnibus. He liked the movement of the huge commercial city'.

Lenin returned again in 1903 and stayed with Krupskaya, his wife, at number **30 Holford Square** (see map on page 93), Finsbury, off the King's Cross Road, ten minutes walk from the station, for the second Congress of the Russian Social Democratic Labour Party, and in 1943 the Russian Ambassador unveiled a monument opposite. The house was destroyed by bombs during the Second World War, and the Square disappeared after 1945, when the area was replanned. It was at the second Congress that the Russian Social Democratic Party split into the two wings

Stepnick, had arrived too, and five years later Edward Bernstein, who was to become a leader of German 'revisionist' Marxism, began a ten year spell in London which he finally left very reluctantly.

Stepnick, whose philosophy was completely different from that of Marx, though it influenced Morris, prophesied that socialist revolution might come to Russia: 'supposing socialism is not entirely a dream,' he wrote in 1888, 'of all European nations, the Russians, providing they become a free nation, have the best opportunity of realising it.'

The architect of the Bolshevik Revolution in Russia in 1917, Lenin, was himself, of course, an exile in London, sharing an editorial office in 1901–2 in Clerkenwell Green (numbers 37/38, now Marx House) with Henry Quelch, one of the leaders of the Social Democratic Federation. He published there a series of issues of *Iskra*, the Russian Social Democratic newspaper, numbers 22 to 38, which was set up at a little Russian printer's shop in the East End. According to his

Marx House, Clerkenwell Green

Holford Square (now demolished), Islington where Lenin lived in 1903. Number 30 is in the centre of the terrace

The plaque which commemorated Lenin's stay in Holford Square

Lenin in 1918

of Bolshevik (majority) and Menshevik (minority) elements, the former led by Lenin, the latter by Trotsky. A split with world-shattering implications in later years.

There is a plaque to Lenin, however, in **Great Percy Street** (see map opposite) where he stayed at the back of what is now the Royal Scot Hotel, for the third Congress in 1905. He was also in London for the fifth Congress in 1907, which was held at the Brotherhood Church, Southgate Road, Islington, now demolished and replaced by a factory. (No one knows where the second and third Congresses were held.) Lenin was also in London briefly in 1908 and 1911 – the last time staying at 6 Oakley Square, NW1, near Mornington Crescent. He also visited the British Museum and the 'Communist Club', successor to the German Workers' Education Society, at 107 Charlotte Street. This was closed down following a police raid in 1918.

There is no evidence that Lenin interested himself in the details of British politics. Yet it is from an analysis of British imperialism that he drew conclusions which were to be as influential as those which Marx had drawn from British capitalism sixty years earlier.

Marx's ideas have now spread far beyond his adopted London. They serve as the ideology of one third of the world's people. In some countries they are a new secular religion, the basis of state power rather than revolution, for the withering away of the state which Marx prophesied, has not come about.

His ideas are even more controversial now than they were in his own lifetime, and there are so many varieties of 'Marxists' that he could not have recognised all of them.

CLERKENWELL GREEN

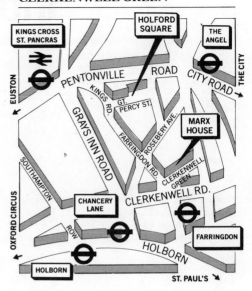

How to get there:

Marx House, Clerkenwell Green, EC1: by underground to Farringdon Station (Circle and Metropolitan lines)
by bus – routes: **63, 55, 19, 171**
Holford Square no longer exists. It was bombed in the Second World War.
Great Percy Street, WC1: by underground to King's Cross Station (Northern, Victoria, Metropolitan and Circle lines); Angel Station (Northern line)
by bus – routes: **19, 38, 63, 168a, 171, 172, 221, 259**
Oakley Square, NW1: by underground to Mornington Crescent Station (Northern line) closed on Saturdays and Sundays.
by bus – routes: **68, 24, 27, 29, 134, 137, 253**
Opening times: Marx Memorial Library, Marx House, Clerkenwell Green, EC1: Monday and Friday 2–6.30p.m. Tuesdays, Wednesdays and Thursdays 2–9p.m. Saturday 11–1p.m. Closed Sundays, Christmas week and all Public Holidays.

Index

Numbers given in *italics*, refer to illustrations